Recreational
Bicycle Trails
of
Minnesota

An American Bike Trails Publication

Recreational
Bicycle Trails of Minnesota

Published by   American Bike Trails
1157 S. Milwaukee Avenue
Libertyville, IL 60048

Created by   Ray Hoven

Design by   Mary C. Rumpsa

Table of Contents

Introduction

Southern Minnesota

Minneapolis/St. Paul Area
Metro

Northwest Metro

Table of Contents (Continued)

Minneapolis/St. Paul Area
Southwest Metro

Northwest Metro

Northern Minnesota

Appendices & Indexes

How To Use This Book

T his book provides a comprehensive, easy-to-use quick reference to the many off-road trails throughout Minnesota. It contains over 50 detailed trail maps, plus overviews covering the state sectionally, organized by north, south and Twin Cities metro area. Trails are listed alphabetically within each section. The sectional overviews are grouped near the front, with a section cross-referencing counties and towns to trails in the back. Each trail map includes such helpful features as location and access, trail facilities, nearby communities and their populations.

Terms Used

Bicycle Trail	An off-road path designated as open to bicycling.
Bikeway	A shoulder, street or sidewalk recommended as a bicycle route.
Alternate Bike Trail	An off-road trail other than the one featured on a map illustration.
Directions	Describes by way of directions and distances, how to get to the trail areas from roads and nearby communities.
DNR	Department of Natural Resources
Forest	Typically encompasses a dense growth of trees and underbrush covering a large tract.
Length	Expressed in miles. Round trip mileage is normally indicated for loops.
Map	Illustrative representation of a geographic area, such as a state, section, forest, park or trail complex.
Park	A tract of land generally including woodlands and open areas.

Types of Biking

Mountain	Fat-tired bikes are recommended. Ride may be generally flat but then with a soft, rocky or wet surface.
Leisure	Off-road gentle ride. Surface is generally paved or screened.
Tour	Riding on roads with motorized traffic or on road shoulders.

Riding Tips

¤ Pushing in gears that are too high can push knees beyond their limits. Avoid extremes by pedaling faster rather than shifting into a higher gear.

¤ Keeping your elbows bent, changing your hand position frequently and wearing bicycle gloves all help to reduce the numbness or pain in the palm of the hand from long-distance riding.

¤ Keep you pedal rpms up on an uphill so you have reserve power if you lose speed.

¤ Stay in a high-gear on a level surface, placing pressure on the pedals and resting on the handle bars and saddle.

¤ Lower your center of gravity on a long or steep downhill run by using the quick release seat post binder and dropping the saddle height down.

¤ Brake intermittently on a rough surface.

¤ Wear proper equipment. Wear a helmet that is approved by the Snell Memorial Foundation or the American National Standards Institute. Look for one of their stickers inside the helmet.

¤ Use a lower tire inflation pressure for riding on unpaved surfaces. The lower pressure will provide better tire traction and a more comfortable ride.

¤ Apply your brakes gradually to maintain control on loose gravel or soil.

¤ Ride only on trails designated for bicycles or in areas where you have the permission of the landowner.

¤ Be courteous to hikers or horseback riders on the trail, they have the right of way.

¤ Leave riding trails in the condition you found them. Be sensitive to the environment. Properly dispose of your trash. If you open a gate, close it behind you.

¤ Don't carry items or attach anything to your bicycle that might hinder your vision or control.

¤ Don't wear anything that restricts your hearing.

¤ Don't carry extra clothing where it can hang down and jam in a wheel.

Explanation of Symbols

ROUTES

▬▬▬▬	Biking Trail
▬▬▬▬	Bikeway
▬ ▬ ▬ ▬	Alternate Bike Trail
▪•▪•▪•▪	Undeveloped Trail
▬ ▬ ▬ ▬	Alternate Use Trail
= = = =	Planned Trail
▬▬▬▬	Roadway

TRAIL USES

🚵	Mountain Biking
🚲	Leisure Biking
🛼	In Line Skating
🎿	(X-C) Cross-Country Skiing
🚶	Hiking
🐴	Horseback Riding
🛷	Snowmobiling

FACILITIES

🔧	Bicycle Service
⛺	Camping
➕	First Aid
❓	Info
🛏	Lodging
🅿	Parking
🏕	Picnic
🍴	Refreshments
🚻	Restrooms
🏠	Shelter
🚰	Water
MF	Multi Facilities Available

Refreshments   First Aid
Telephone   Picnic
Restrooms   Lodging

ROAD RELATED SYMBOLS

45	Interstate Highway
45	U.S. Highway
45	State Highway
45	County Highway

AREA DESCRIPTIONS

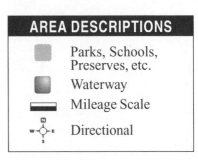

	Parks, Schools, Preserves, etc.
	Waterway
	Mileage Scale
	Directional

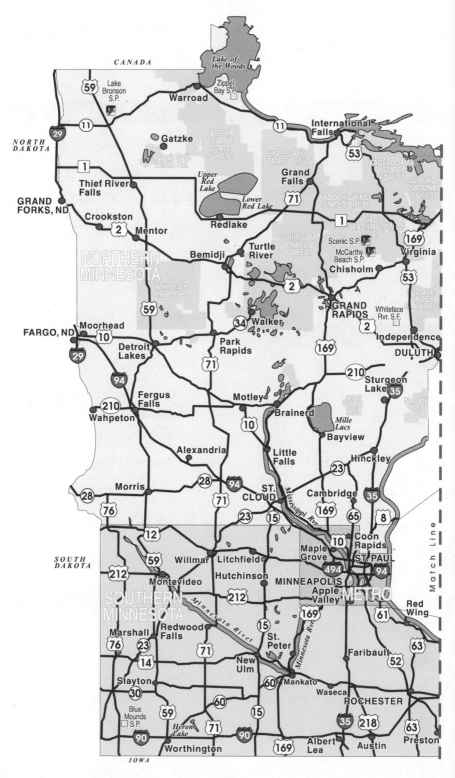

State of Minnesota

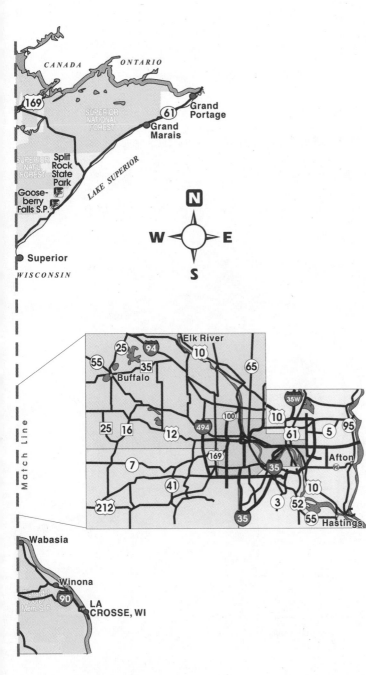

Southern Minnesota

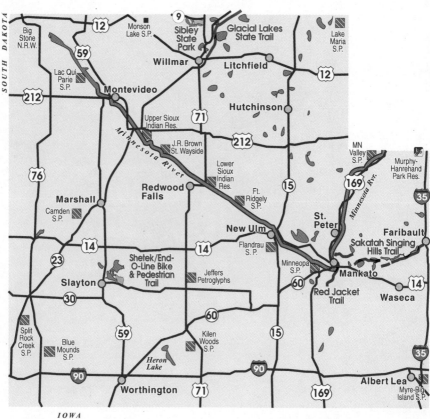

Southern Minnesota Science & Nature Centers

Quarry Hill Nature Center—701 Silver Creek Rd NE, Rochester • Open year round, M-Sat 8-4:30; Sun 12-4:30. Caves, quarry, stream & trails. Free admission & parking. Located near 4th St S & Co Rd 22 (E Circle Dr).

Museum of Natural History—Dept of Biology, SW State Univ., Marshall • Open M-F 8-4:30 during academic year. Flora and fauna exhibits of southwestern MN. Free admission & parking. Located N of Hwy 19 on Hwy 23.

Dale A Gardner Aerospace Museum & Learning Center—112 N Main, Sherburn • Summer, M-F 1-5, Sat 9-5, or by appointment. Suit worn by Gardner on shuttle, heat shield tiles, stardome, library & space videos. Free admission & parking. Take exit 87 at I-90 & 4.

J.C. Hormel Nature Center—Box 673, Austin • M-Sat 9-5 (closed 12-1) Sun 1-5. Woods, prairie. .5 mi of asphalt trail allows wheelchairs, strollers, etc. into preserve. 278 acres with 7.5 mi of walking trails. Free admission & parking. 1/4 mi N of I-90E on exit 218.

Southern Minnesota Attractions

Big Stone Wildlife Refuge—25 NW 2nd St, Ortonville • May-Sept sunrise-sunset. Auto tours & foot trails through refuge. Free, located SE from Hwys 75 & 12, 2+ mi.

Alexander Ramsey Park—Hwy 19, Redwood Falls • Open year round, until 10pm daily. Largest municipal park in MN with hiking & ski trails, playgrounds, campsites & an exercise course.

Big Stone County Historical Museum—RR 2, Box 31, Orton-ville • Year round, T-F 11-4 May-Sept: S&S 1-4. Historic boat, Native American photographer Roland Reed photos, caskets; historic flags & more. Adults $2, Free parking. Junction of US 12 & 75.

Freeborn County Historical Museum & Pioneer Village—1031 Bridge Ave N, Albert Lea • Museum, library, 1880s village, log cabins, school, church, blacksmith, PO & shops. Open year round. Adults $3. Free parking. 2 mi S of I-90, near fairgrounds, Exit #157.

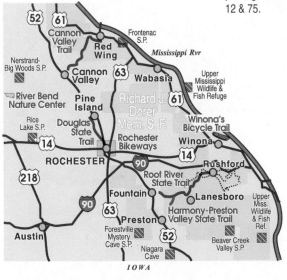

Cannon Valley Trail

Trail Length	19.7 miles
Surface	Asphalt
Uses	Leisure bicycling, cross country skiing, in-line skating, hiking
Location & Setting	The Cannon Valley Trail runs from Cannon Falls to Red Wing on an abandoned railroad line in southeastern Minnesota. There are overhanging cliffs near Cannon Falls, and the scenery is diverse and spectacular. The setting includes woods, river views, bluffs and small communities.
Information	Cannon Falls City Hall (507) 263-3954 306 West Mill Street Cannon Falls, MN 55009
Counties	Goodhue

WELCH—The trail passes a downhill ski resort. Welch is a small village 1/3 mile north of the Welch station access (look for signs on trail). Bicycle and canoe/tube rental is available. Camping nearby at Hidden Valley Campground.

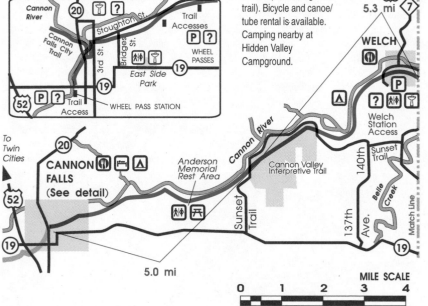

CANNON FALLS

5.0 mi

MILE SCALE
0 1 2 3 4

CANNON FALLS—*pop. 3,300* Western Trailhead is located at the ballpark on E. Stoughton St., but a trail extension continues on as the Cannon Falls City Trail for approximately 2 miles near Hwys. 19 & 20. There is parking at the trailhead, and ample facilities and shopping can be found within Cannon Falls.

Wheel passes are required if bicycling or in-line skating and age 18 or older. Available at trailside self purchase stations ($2.00/day or $10.00/season).

Goodhue County Historical Society— 1166 Oak St, Red Wing, MN 55066 • Archaeological & geological exhibits; pottery collection, Dakota tribal history. Fashions, medicine & immigration period.

Cannon Valley Trail Office
(507) 263-5843

Cannon Falls Chamber of Commerce
(507) 263-2289

Red Wing Chamber of Commerce
(612) 388-4719

Emergency Assistance
Dial 911

ROUTE SLIP	INCREMENT	TOTAL
Red Wing		
Hwy. 61	4.7	4.7
Belle Creek	3.6	8.3
Welch Station	1.4	9.7
Sunset Trail	5.0	14.7
Anderson Rest Area	1.2	15.9
Cannon Falls	3.8	19.7

MILE SCALE

0   1   2   3   4

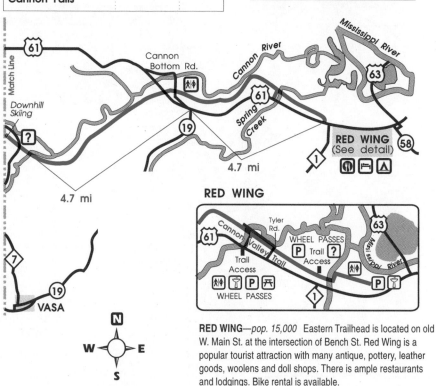

RED WING—*pop. 15,000* Eastern Trailhead is located on old W. Main St. at the intersection of Bench St. Red Wing is a popular tourist attraction with many antique, pottery, leather goods, woolens and doll shops. There is ample restaurants and lodgings. Bike rental is available.

Cannon Valley Trail

Douglas State Trail

🚲 🎿 🛼 🎧 🏂 🏃

Trail Length	12.5 miles
Surface	Asphalt (with a separate turf threadway)
Uses	Leisure bicycling, cross country skiing, in-line skating, horseback riding, snowmobiling, jogging
Location & Setting	The Douglas State Trails is multi-use and was developed on abandoned, railroad bed. The trail travels from northwest Rochester, through the town of Douglas, and ends at Pine Island.
Information	Douglas State Trail (507) 285-7176 2300 Silver Circle Road, NE Rochester, MN 55906
Counties	Olmsted

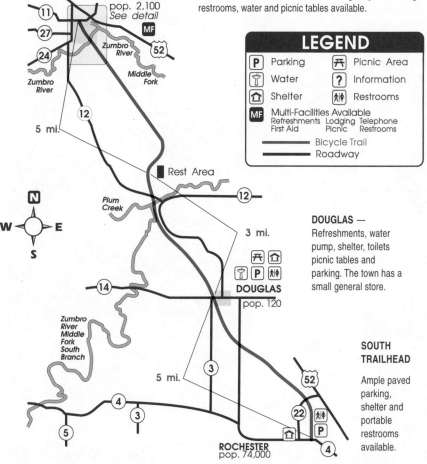

NORTH TRAILHEAD—Trail ends at Highway 11. Parking, restrooms, water and picnic tables available.

LEGEND

P	Parking	🎪	Picnic Area
🚰	Water	?	Information
🏠	Shelter	🚻	Restrooms
MF	Multi-Facilities Available Refreshments Lodging Telephone First Aid Picnic Restrooms		

——— Bicycle Trail
——— Roadway

DOUGLAS — Refreshments, water pump, shelter, toilets picnic tables and parking. The town has a small general store.

SOUTH TRAILHEAD

Ample paved parking, shelter and portable restrooms available.

PINE ISLAND

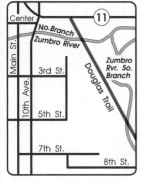

DOUGLAS STATE TRAIL

The trail is wide and in excellent condition, but there is the need to cross several country gravel roads. Enroute you will cross the Zumbro River and Plum Creek on wide refurbished bridges. Mid access: Douglas on CR 14 and exit off Hwy. 52. There is a large parking lot, shelter, water and restrooms at milepost 5 from Rochester.

PINE ISLAND— elev. 1,004

Washroom, shelter, picnic tables, parking.
Restaurants and lodging are available in the area.

Douglas State Trail

Red Jacket Trail

Trail Length	5.6 miles
Surface	Paved
Uses	Leisure bicycling, cross country skiing, in-line skating, jogging
Location & Setting	The Red Jacket Trail is built on abandoned railroad bed with its trail head at West High School in Mankato. The trail continues southwest where it ends at County Road 9 just west of County Road 33. There is a railroad trestle as it crosses Highway 66. Setting is urban and countryside.

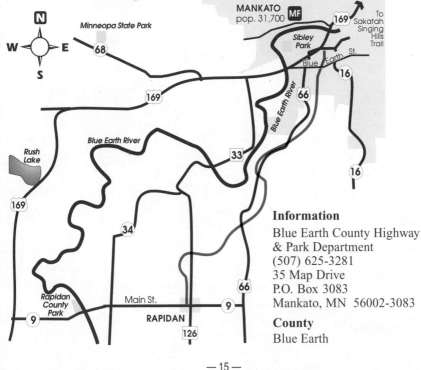

Information
Blue Earth County Highway & Park Department
(507) 625-3281
35 Map Drive
P.O. Box 3083
Mankato, MN 56002-3083

County
Blue Earth

Glacial Lakes State Trail

Trail Length	36.0 miles (includes 18 miles planned)
Surface	Asphalt: 12 miles between Willmar & New London Crushed granite: 6 miles between New London & Hawick Undeveloped: 18 miles between Hawick & Richmond
Uses	Leisure bicycling, cross country skiing, in-line skating, snowmobiling, horseback riding, hiking
Location & Setting	The Glacial Lakes State Trail is built on abandoned railroad bed and is located in southwestern Minnesota between Willmar and Richmond. The topography is rolling and it cuts across the border between western tall grass prairie and eastern deciduous forest. Farmland, virgin prairie remnants and scattered wood lots.
Information	Minnesota Department of Natural Resources (612) 296-6157 *or (800) 766-6000 in Minnesota* 500 Lafayette Road St. Paul, MN 55155-4040
Counties	Kandiyohi, Stearns

Parking Facilities—

Willmar - take Highway 12 east to County Road 9. Turn left (north) and go 2 miles to the Civic Center.

Spicer - junction of Highway 23 and County Road 10. Parking is off 23.

New London - From Highway 23, follow Highway 9 north to parking and public water access on the east.

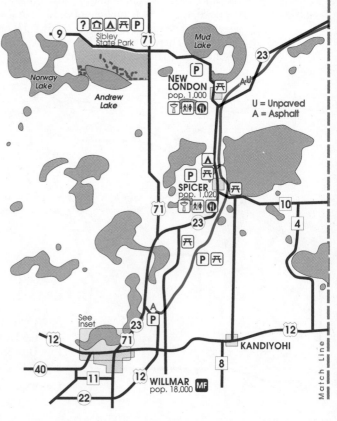

MILE SCALE
0 1 2 3 4

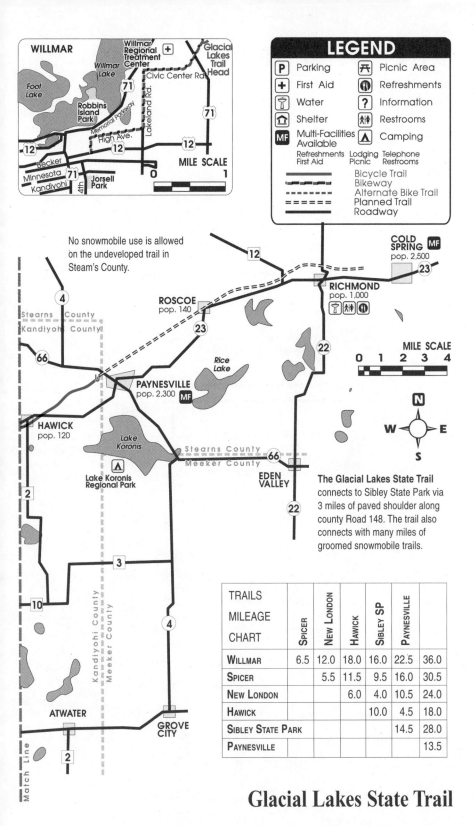

Glacial Lakes State Trail

TRAILS MILEAGE CHART	Spicer	New London	Hawick	Sibley SP	Paynesville	
Willmar	6.5	12.0	18.0	16.0	22.5	36.0
Spicer		5.5	11.5	9.5	16.0	30.5
New London			6.0	4.0	10.5	24.0
Hawick				10.0	4.5	18.0
Sibley State Park					14.5	28.0
Paynesville						13.5

River Bend Nature Center

🚴 ⛷ 🚶

Trail Length	8.0 miles
Surface	Packed dirt
Uses	Leisure bicycling, cross country skiing, hiking
Location & Setting	The River Bend Nature Center is located in Faribault about 50 miles south of Minneapolis/St. Paul. The setting includes forest, prairie, wetland and riverbank.
Information	River Bend Nature Center (507) 332-7151 P.O. Box 265 Faribault, MN 55021
Counties	Rice

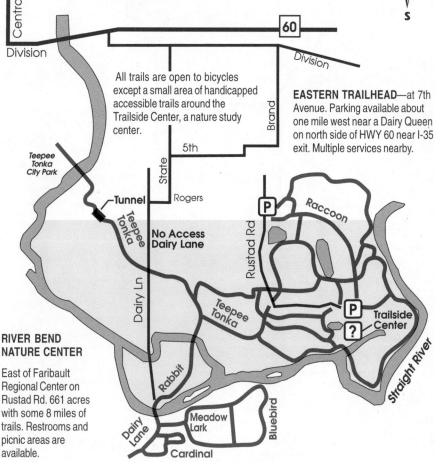

To **FARIBAULT**, pop. 17,085. (about 50 miles south of the Twin Cities)
See Sakatah Singing Hill State Trail map for inset of Faribault

Central
Division

60

Division

All trails are open to bicycles except a small area of handicapped accessible trails around the Trailside Center, a nature study center.

EASTERN TRAILHEAD—at 7th Avenue. Parking available about one mile west near a Dairy Queen on north side of HWY 60 near I-35 exit. Multiple services nearby.

Brand

5th

Teepee
Tonka
City Park

State

Tunnel   Rogers

Teepee
Tonka

**No Access
Dairy Lane**

P   Raccoon

Rustad Rd

Dairy Ln

Teepee
Tonka

P   Trailside
Center
?

**RIVER BEND
NATURE CENTER**

East of Faribault Regional Center on Rustad Rd. 661 acres with some 8 miles of trails. Restrooms and picnic areas are available.

Rabbit

Dairy
Lane

Meadow
Lark

Bluebird

Straight River

Cardinal

Rochester Trails & Bikeways

Trail Length	Over 100.0 miles
Surface	Asphalt paths and designated streets
Uses	Leisure bicycling, in-line skating, jogging
Location & Setting	Rochester is located in southeastern Minnesota. It has an excellent system of bicycle trails along the waterways and through it's many parks.
Information	City of Rochester(507) 281-6160 403 East Center Rochester, MN 55904
Counties	Olmsted

Map on following page

Bicycle licenses are required and are available at local license bureaus and at several bike shops.

Bicycle signs identify off-road trails, on-road routes and designated bike lanes.

Bicycle parking racks are provided in most municipal lots and at various locations in the downtown area.

Rochester Area Attractions

Heritage House of Rochester—225 First Av NW Rochester, MN 55903
• Located in Central Park, an 1856 town square. Exhibits life of midwestern family 100 years ago, restored house authentically furnished with antiques, quilts, dolls, garden, etc.

Olmsted County History Center—1195 Co Rd 22 SW, Rochester, MN 55902
• History of Rochester and surrounding area; research library/archives with over 600,000 maps, photographs, diaries, etc. relating primarily to Olmsted County and southeastern MN

BIKE ROUTE SIGNS identify on-road routes usually connecting or leading to off-road facilities.

BIKE PATH SIGNS identify off-road facilities.

BIKE LANE SIGNS identify a designated lane for bicycles usually on the right side of the roadway.

Rochester Trails & Bikeways

ROCHESTER
pop. 75,000

MAYO CLINIC

The largest medical complex in the world, the Mayo Clinic is reflected in it's diagnostic resources, educational and research facilities.

There is a twenty minute informational film shown weekdays at 10:00 a.m. and again at 2:00 p.m. in the Judd Hall subway level of the Mayo Building.

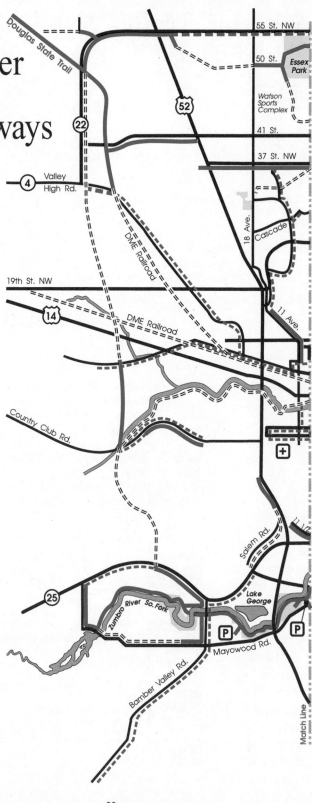

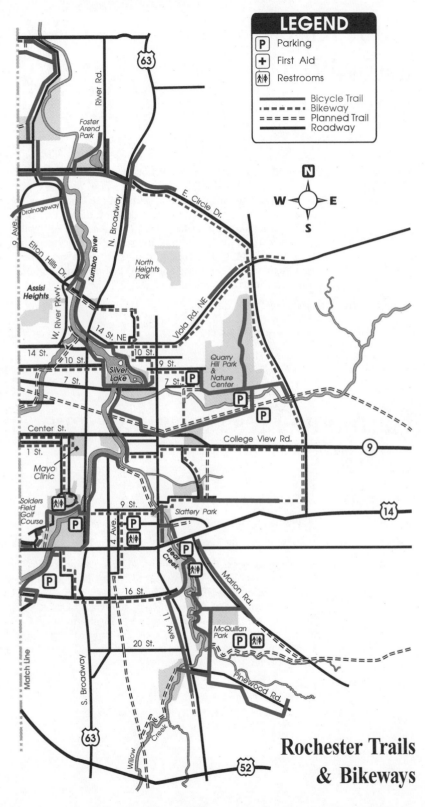

Rochester Trails & Bikeways

Root River Trail

Trail Length	35.3 miles
Surface	Asphalt
Uses	Leisure bicycling, cross country skiing, in-line skating, hiking
Location & Setting	Located in southeastern Minnesota between Fountain and 5.8 miles east of Rushford, the Root River Trail provides outstanding views of the soaring limestone bluffs of the Root River Valley. It was developed on abandoned railroad grade. Wildlife is abundant and sightings of wild turkey, deer, hawks and turkey vultures are common. Historical buildings and rural communities along the trail provide sites of interest to trail users. Services to be found include campgrounds, bed and breakfast inns, restaurants, museums, outfitters and unique stores.
Information	Historic Bluff County (800) 428-2030 P.O. Box 609, 45 Center Street E Harmony, MN 55939
Counties	Fillmore, Houston

Harmony–Preston Valley State Trail

Trail Length	18.0 miles
Surface	Asphalt - 5.5 miles; remainder - undeveloped
Uses	Leisure bicycling, cross country skiing, in-line skating, hiking
Location & Setting	The trail connects the communities of Harmony and Preston with the Root River Trail. The northern two-thirds of the Harmony—Preston Valley State Trail will follow and or cross Watson Creek, the South Branch of the Root River, and Camp Creek, passing through a variety of wooded areas and farmland on an abandoned railroad grad. The southern third of the trail between Preston and Harmony will climb out of the valley and travel along a ridge line between valleys.
Information	Historic Bluff County (800) 428-2030 P.O. Box 609, 45 Center Street E Harmony, MN 55939
Counties	Fillmore

FOUNTAIN

Western Trailhead. Parking lot is adjacent to the city ball field, toilets available.

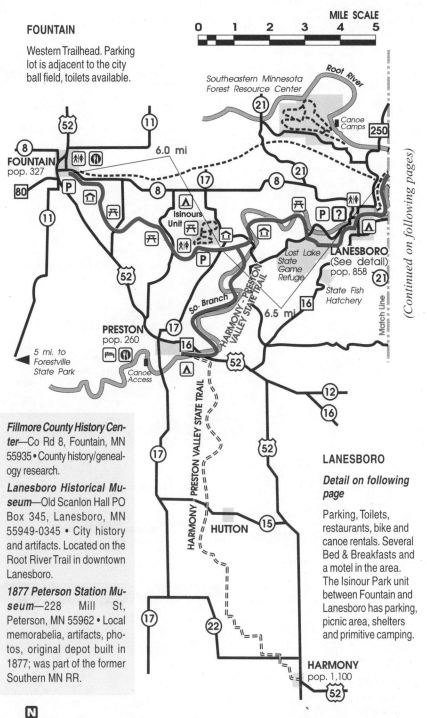

(Continued on following pages)

Fillmore County History Center—Co Rd 8, Fountain, MN 55935 • County history/genealogy research.

Lanesboro Historical Museum—Old Scanlon Hall PO Box 345, Lanesboro, MN 55949-0345 • City history and artifacts. Located on the Root River Trail in downtown Lanesboro.

1877 Peterson Station Museum—228 Mill St, Peterson, MN 55962 • Local memorabelia, artifacts, photos, original depot built in 1877; was part of the former Southern MN RR.

LANESBORO

Detail on following page

Parking, Toilets, restaurants, bike and canoe rentals. Several Bed & Breakfasts and a motel in the area. The Isinour Park unit between Fountain and Lanesboro has parking, picnic area, shelters and primitive camping.

Root River Trail
& Harmony-Preston Valley State Trail

Root River Trail

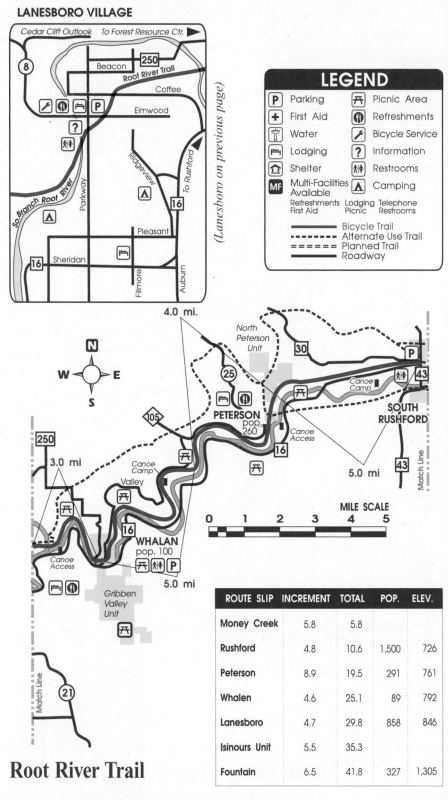

North Peterson Unit

25 · 30 · 105 · PETERSON pop. 260 · Canoe Camp · Canoe Access · 16 · 43 · SOUTH RUSHFORD · Match Line

250 · 3.0 mi · Canoe Camp · Valley · 16 · WHALAN pop. 100 · Canoe Access · Gribben Valley Unit · 4.0 mi. · 5.0 mi · 5.0 mi

Match Line · 21

MILE SCALE

0 1 2 3 4 5

ROUTE SLIP	INCREMENT	TOTAL	POP.	ELEV.
Money Creek	5.8	5.8		
Rushford	4.8	10.6	1,500	726
Peterson	8.9	19.5	291	761
Whalen	4.6	25.1	89	792
Lanesboro	4.7	29.8	858	846
Isinours Unit	5.5	35.3		
Fountain	6.5	41.8	327	1,305

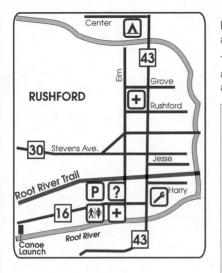

RUSHFORD—Parking, toilets, restaurants, picnic area and canoe rentals near the old train depot at the trailhead.

There are 46 bridges along the Root River Trail; one is approximately 500 feet long. In addition to biking, there is ample opportunities for canoeing or fishing.

PARKING AVAILABLE AT:

Fountain—From Highway 52 take County Road 8 about one mile to parking lot by city park/softball field.

Preston—Highway 52 to Fillmore St. (same as Co. 12), approximately 1/2 mile to the parking lot.

Lanesboro—Parking is along streets, at the parking lot by the Community Center and Sylvan Park. Overflow parking is being developed by the softball field.

Rushford—From Highway 16, turn north on Elm Street, go one block Parking lot is by depot.

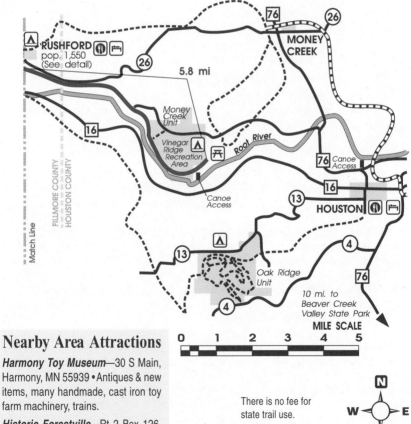

Nearby Area Attractions

Harmony Toy Museum—30 S Main, Harmony, MN 55939 • Antiques & new items, many handmade, cast iron toy farm machinery, trains.

Historic Forestville—Rt 2 Box 126, Preston, MN 55965 • Village restored to 1899; store/post office, Thomas J. Meighen's residence; costumed guides depicting daily lives.

There is no fee for state trail use.

Root River Trail

Sakatah Singing Hills State Trail

🚲 🎿 🛼

Trail Length	39 miles
Surface	Asphalt
Uses	Leisure bicycling, cross country skiing, in-line skating
Location & Setting	The Sakatah Singing Hills Trails is located between Mankato and Faribault in south central Minnesota It was developed on abandoned railroad grade. This level trail wanders pastures, farmland, several lakes, and a forested park.
Information	Sakatah Singing Hills Trail (507) 267-4772 Elysian Wayside P.O. Box 11 Elysian, MN 56028
	River Bend Nature Center (507) 32-7151 P.O. Box 265 Faribault, MN 55021
	Mankato Chamber of Commerce (507) 345-4772 P.O. Box 999 Mankato, MN 56002
Counties	Rice, LeSueur, Blue Earth

Sakatah Singing Hills State Trail Area Attractions

Alexander Faribault House—121st Ave NE, Faribault, MN 55021-5226 • Historic 1853 residence, period furnishings, some original belongings; Alexander Faribault helped establish Minnesota as a state.

Blue Earth County Historical Society—416 Cherry St., Mankato, MN 56001 • Located at the Heritage Center; museum hightlights settlement, history and culture of Blue Earth County and Mankato, with artifacts from Blue Earth County Historical Society Collection.

MN Valley Regional Library-Maud Hart Lovelace Collection—100 Main St E., Mankato, MN 56001 • Children's books items of interest including large mural, original drawings, autographed collection, slide-tape presentation and many items of memorabilia.

Le Sueur Cty History Society Museum—2nd & Frank St., Elysian, MN 56028 • County history; famous area artists; genealogy center; post office, county schoolroom, military exhibit, church room.

Le Sueur City Museum—709 2nd St N., Le Sueur, MN 56058 • Located in the old Union School building, built in 1872, burned down and rebuilt in 1911. Features include 75 years of Green Giant Company history; veterinary office with pharmacy, old hotel, musical instruments, paintings by local artists, high school class photos, family research center, agricultural & military exhibits.

R. D. Hubbard House—606 Broad St S., Mankato, MN 56001 • Victorian 1871 Second Empire mansion, carriage house, formal gardens.

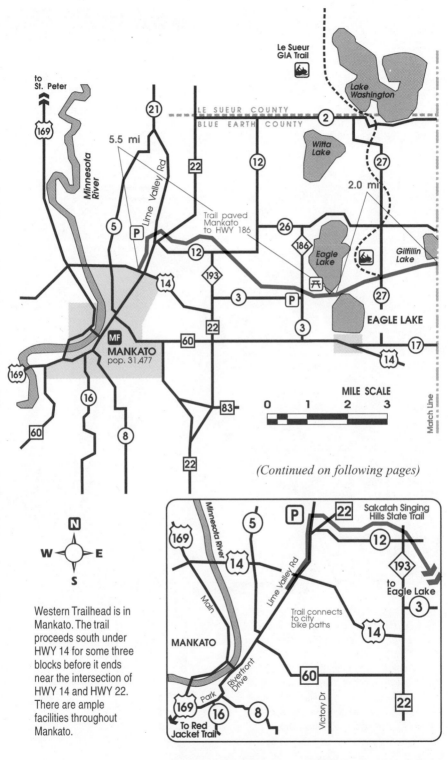

Western Trailhead is in Mankato. The trail proceeds south under HWY 14 for some three blocks before it ends near the intersection of HWY 14 and HWY 22. There are ample facilities throughout Mankato.

(Continued on following pages)

Sakatah Singing Hills State Trail

The trail parallels HWY 60 just north of the road as you proceed west from Elysian. Food and lodging available in town. Parking, picnic area, and shelter available in park.

The town of Madison Lake has a historic station house. There is parking, food, and gift stores nearby.

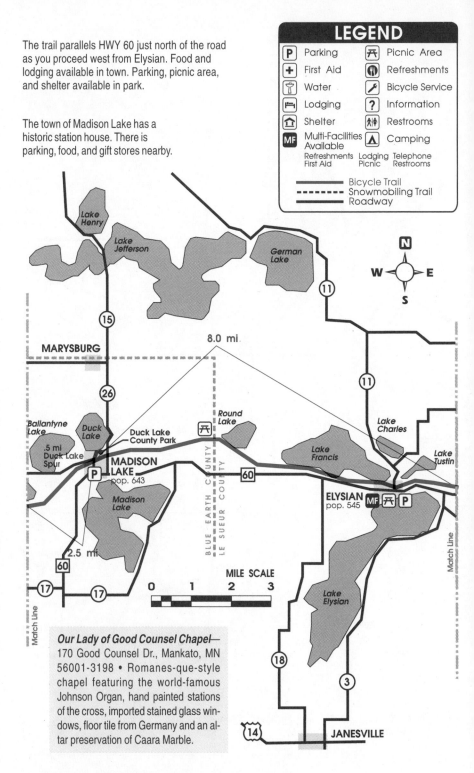

LEGEND

P	Parking	🏕	Picnic Area
+	First Aid	🍴	Refreshments
🚰	Water	🔧	Bicycle Service
🛏	Lodging	?	Information
🏠	Shelter	🚻	Restrooms
MF	Multi-Facilities Available	⛺	Camping

Refreshments   Lodging   Telephone
First Aid   Picnic   Restrooms

——— Bicycle Trail
------- Snowmobiling Trail
——— Roadway

N W E S

MARYSBURG

8.0 mi

Lake Henry
Lake Jefferson
German Lake

Ballantyne Lake
Duck Lake
.5 mi Duck Lake Spur
Duck Lake County Park
Round Lake

MADISON LAKE pop. 643
Madison Lake

BLUE EARTH COUNTY
LE SUEUR COUNTY

Lake Charles
Lake Francis
Lake Tustin

ELYSIAN pop. 545

2.5 mi

MILE SCALE
0   1   2   3

Lake Elysian

Our Lady of Good Counsel Chapel— 170 Good Counsel Dr., Mankato, MN 56001-3198 • Romanes-que-style chapel featuring the world-famous Johnson Organ, hand painted stations of the cross, imported stained glass windows, floor tile from Germany and an altar preservation of Caara Marble.

JANESVILLE

Match Line

Sakatah Singing Hills State Trail

A one mile secondary bike path provides access into Morristown. As you enter town, observe the historic old mill and dam. Restaurant and groceries available.

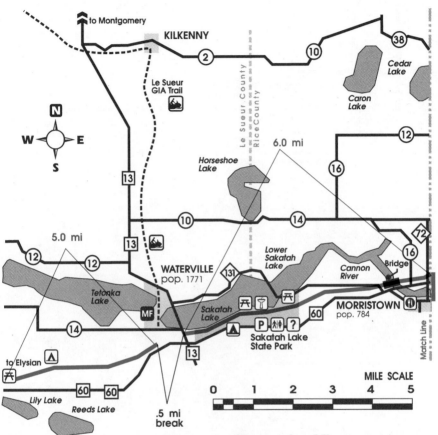

(Continued on following page)

The trail ends east of Waterville and picks up again west at Pick Street just a little north of Common St. Enter Waterville by car by exiting HWY 60 north onto HWY 13. Parking, restaurants, restrooms, and lodging available.

ROUTE SLIP	INCREMENT	TOTAL	ELEV.
Faribault			999
Warsaw	6.5	5.5	
HWY 72	2.5	9.0	1000
(to Morristown)	(1.0)		
Trail Break	.5		
Waterville	6.0	15.0	1010
Elysian (HWY 11)	5.5	20.5	
Madison Lake (HWY26)	7.5	28.0	1050
Eagle Lake	4.5	32.5	
Mankato	5.5	38.0	794

Sakatah Singing Hills State Trail

FARIBAULT

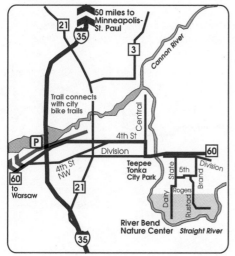

FARIBAULT

50 miles to
Minneapolis-
St. Paul

21
35
3

Cannon River

Trail connects
with city
bike trails

Central

4th St
Division

4th St
NW

60
to
Warsaw

21

Teepee
Tonka
City Park

Dairy
State
5th
Rustad
Rogers
Brand
Division

60

35

River Bend
Nature Center   Straight River

Rice County Historical Society Museum—1814 2nd Ave NW, Faribault, MN 55021 • Rice County history from early American Indian times to Rice County pioneers, turn-of-the-century Main St, slide show; nearby log cabin, one-room schoolhouse, historic frame church, two agricultural and industrial buildings, genealogical research.

Trail access near west end of Cannon Lake. Parking, restroom, and picnic facilities.

Roberds
Lake

99
21
35
3

Rice Co.
GIA Trails

Cannon River

11

6.5 mi

38

P

60

60

Cedar
Lake

Wells
Lake

FARIBAULT
pop. 17,085

MF

12

12

Straight River

60

21

Rice Co.
GIA Trails

13

Cannon
Lake

35

45

71

13

Harris Trail

Shager
Cty.
Park

WARSAW
Bridge

Rice Co.
GIA Trails

MILE SCALE

0   1   2   3   4   5

1.0 mi
Morristown
Spur

15

2.5 mi

N
W   E
S

LEGEND

P	Parking	🎑	Picnic Area
+	First Aid	🍺	Refreshments
🚰	Water	🔧	Bicycle Service
🛏	Lodging	?	Information
🏠	Shelter	🚻	Restrooms
MF	Multi-Facilities Available	⛺	Camping

Refreshments Lodging Telephone
First Aid   Picnic   Restrooms

Bicycle Trail
Snowmobiling Trail
Roadway

Match Line

Sakatah Singing
Hills State Trail

Shetek/End-O-Line Bike & Pedestrian Trail

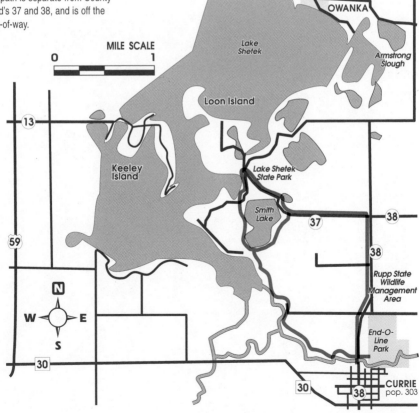

Trail Length	5.7 miles
Surface	Asphalt
Uses	Leisure bicycling, cross country skiing, in-line skating, jogging
Location & Setting	The trail is a loop connecting the town of Currie with Shetek State Park. From Currie, the trail runs north parallel to County Road 38, then west parallel to County Road 37 to Lake Shetek. From there it continues south, then southeast, returning to the starting point at End-O-Line Park. Open area, lakefront.
Information	Murray County Highway Department (507) 836-6327 3051 20th Street Slayton, MN 56172
Counties	Murray

The path is separate from County Road's 37 and 38, and is off the right-of-way.

Sibley State Park

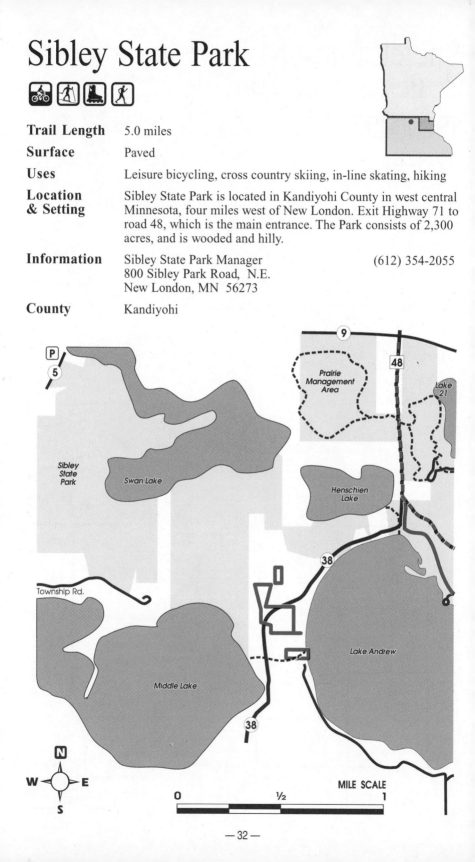

Trail Length	5.0 miles
Surface	Paved
Uses	Leisure bicycling, cross country skiing, in-line skating, hiking
Location & Setting	Sibley State Park is located in Kandiyohi County in west central Minnesota, four miles west of New London. Exit Highway 71 to road 48, which is the main entrance. The Park consists of 2,300 acres, and is wooded and hilly.
Information	Sibley State Park Manager (612) 354-2055 800 Sibley Park Road, N.E. New London, MN 56273
County	Kandiyohi

Prairie Management Area

Lake 21

Sibley State Park

Swan Lake

Henschien Lake

Township Rd.

38

Lake Andrew

Middle Lake

38

N
W—E
S

MILE SCALE

0 ½ 1

Sibley State Park was named after Henry Hastings Sibley, Minnesota's first governor. The Park is located in an area where the grasslands of the west meet the big woods of the east. Mt. Tom is the highest point within 50 miles, affording an excellent view of surrounding forest, prairie knolls, lakes and farmland.

MILE SCALE

0   ½   1

Facilities include:

18 miles of hiking trail
10 miles of cross-country ski trail
9 miles of horseback riding trail and group camp
6 miles of snowmobile trail
Campsites, picnic area, swimming beach
Canoe rentals
Park store

LEGEND

P	Parking	🛏	Picnic Area
Δ	Camping	?	Information
⌂	Shelter		

——— Bicycle Trail
------- Alternate Use Trail
━━━ Roadway

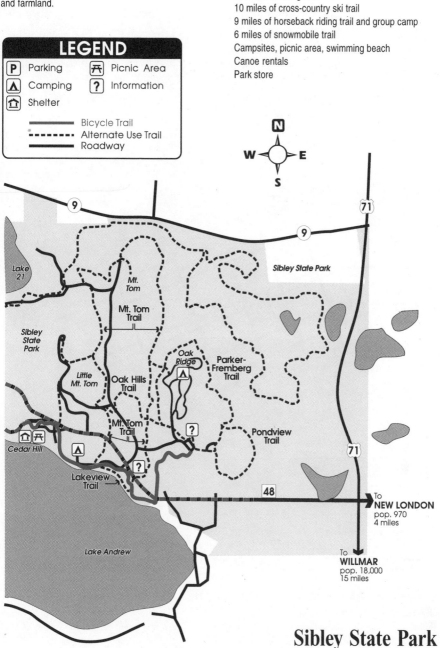

Sibley State Park

Winona's Bicycle Trail

Trail Length	5.3 miles
Surface	Asphalt
Uses	Leisure bicycling, cross country skiing, in-line skating, jogging
Location & Setting	City of Winona in southeastern Minnesota. The trail forms two loops surrounding Lake Winona. The trail head is located at the information center on Huff Road, just east of Highway 61. Open park area some tree shading, continuous lake views.
Information	Winona Visitors Bureau (507) 452-2272 67 Main Street Winona, MN 55987
Counties	Winona

In addition to the bike path, some of the streets in town are designated bike routes. Winona is on the Bike Centennial route and is close to the Root River State Trail and the Great River Trail (in Wisconsin). Bike rentals are available at the bike store on Center Street.

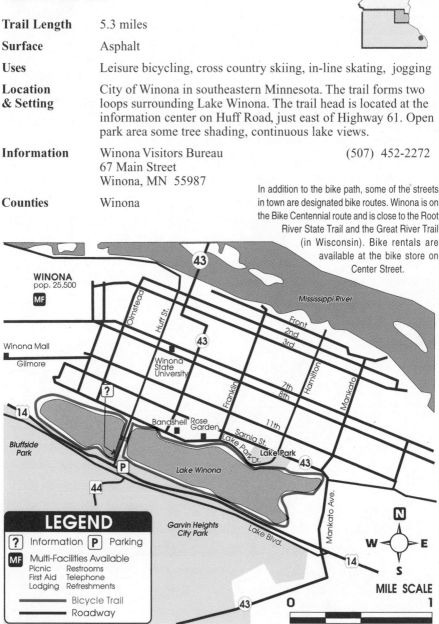

Bunnell House Museum—160 Johnson St., Winona, MN 55987 • Rural gothic wood frame home built in 1850s, overlooks Mississippi River.
Winona County Historical Museum—160 Johnson St, Winona, MN 55987 • American Indian exhibit, county history, Mississippi River history, archives.

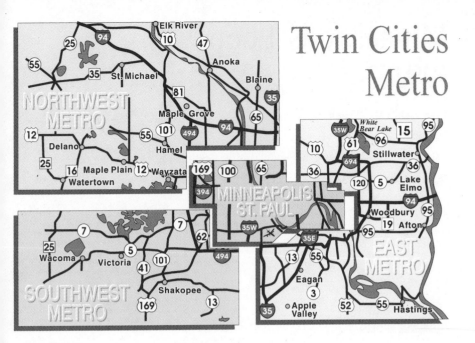

Twin Cities Metro

Minneapolis — St. Paul

USEFUL PHONE NUMBERS FOR THE MINNEAPOLIS—ST. PAUL AREA

EMERGENCY		
	Police, Fire, Sheriff, Medical	911
	Road Condition Information	(612) 296-3076
GENERAL INFORMATION		
City Line	Sports, weather, recreation, restaurants, buses, etc.	(612) 645-6060
The Connection	Restaurants, business, entertainment, sports, live theater	(612) 922-9000
Ticketmaster	Tickets for sporting events, concerts, theater, special events	(612) 989-5151
Time and Weather		(612) 452-2323

Minneapolis Loop

Trail Length	30.0 miles
Surface	Paved
Uses	Leisure bicycling, in-line skating, jogging/hiking
Information	Greater Minneapolis Chamber (612) 370-9132
	Fort Snelling State Park (612) 727-1961
	Assistance Dial 911
Counties	Hennepin

THE MINNEAPOLIS LOOP

Thirty miles long, this urban route shows off the major highlights of the city. It passes by the Walker Art Center/Guthrie Theatre, and the sculpture garden. It travels through Loring Park, along Loring Greenway, by Orchestra Hall and along Nicollet Mall, one of the largest downtown malls in the nation. After crossing the Mississippi River on the Third Ave. Bridge, the route leads to the University of Minnesota (Minneapolis Campus). The route returns to Fort Snelling State Park at the confluence of the Minnesota and Mississippi Rivers.

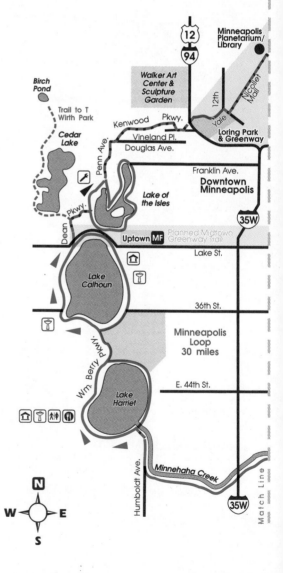

MILE SCALE

0   1

N
W — E
S

ROUTE FROM MINNEAPOLIS/ST. PAUL INTERNATIONAL AIRPORT

Turn left as you come out of the terminal, ride on the sidewalk around the south side of the terminal, then use the road between the Northwest Airline hangers and the Northwest Airlines parking lot. Follow Airport Road, then Frontage Road running south alongside Interstate 494 and State Hwy. 5. Frontage Road ends at Post Road. Turn left onto Post Rd. and cross I494/Hwy. 5. Enter the park on the paved bicycle trail, which leads to the starting point of the Trail Explorer route.

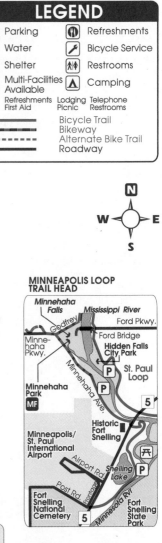

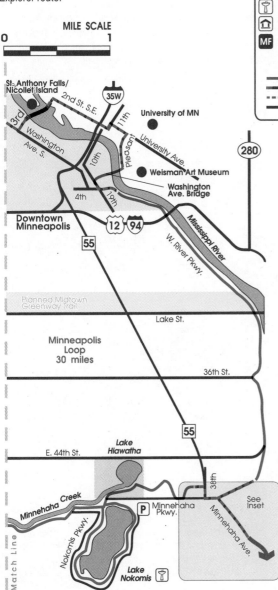

FORT SNELLING STATE PARK ACCESS

Take State Highway 5 to Post Road exit to reach the park. Post Road enters the park and serves as a bicycle route into the airport.

Minneapolis Loop

Midtown Greenway

Trail Length	4.0 miles (planned)
Surface	Paved
Uses	Leisure bicycling, in-line skating, jogging
Location & Setting	The Midtown Greenway will be a long narrow park built all the way across Minneapolis along the 29th Street railroad corridor. The Greenway will include community gardens, play area, nature area, and bordering businesses and housing.
Information	Midtown Greenway Coalition (612) 724-3288 2845 16th Avenue South Minneapolis, MN 55407
Counties	Hennepin

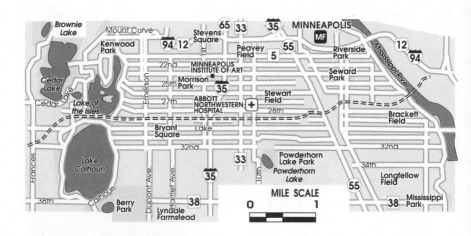

Because the Midtown Greenway is down below street level, bicyclists will be able to travel nonstop as they pass under bridges carrying the city street overhead. The Greenway will be lit at night and plowed in the winter. It will also link up with other planned bikeways connecting with St. Paul to the east and suburbs to the west.

St. Anthony Falls

Trail Length	4.0 miles
Surface	Asphalt
Uses	Leisure bicycling, in-line skating, jogging
Location & Setting	Straddles the Mississippi River between Stone Arch Bridge and Plymouth Avenue in north central Minneapolis. Level and easy with great views of Saint Anthony Falls and the Minneapolis skyline.
Counties	Hennepin

LEGEND

- **P** Parking
- **?** Information
- Bicycle Trail
- Bikeway
- Planned Trail
- Roadway

8th Ave.

BOOM ISLAND PARK

Plymouth Ave.

P

Mississippi River

47

P

NICOLLET ISLAND

Main St.

OUR LADY OF LOURDES
ARD.GODFREY HOUSE
RIVERPLACE

P

52

W. River Pkwy

Hennepin Bridge

Third Ave.

University Ave.

52

ST. ANTHONY MAIN

3rd Ave Bridge

52

HENNEPIN BLUFF PARK

Main St.

394

Hennepin Ave.

VISITOR CENTER ?

ST. ANTHONY FALLS

Stone Arch Bridge

NICOLLET MALL

52

Third St.

Fourth St.

Washington Ave.

Second St.

35W

CONSERVATORY

Lasalle

Third Ave.

Chicago Ave.

Park Ave.

METRODOME

Fifth St.

Eleventh Ave.

BIKE BRIDGE

MILE SCALE

0   ¼   ½

The bikeway over Stone Arch Bridge provides a spectacular view of the Falls. It was these Falls that allowed Minneapolis to lead the world in milling from 1880 to 1930 with the flour mills that sprang up along the river banks.

N
W E
S

INFORMATION ON SELECTED
MINNEAPOLIS PARKS

MINNEHAHA PARKWAY   .   Phone: (612) 661-4800

A parkway with bicycle trails and walking paths stretching from the southeast end of Lake Harriet to Hiawatha Ave. Hours are from 6 a.m. to midnight. Park facilities include biking, creative play areas, hiking, cross-country skiing.

MISSISSIPPI GORGE   Phone: (612) 661-4800

Walking, biking trails on East and West River Parkways from Washington Ave. Bridge to Minnehaha Falls in Minneapolis. Hours on the Minneapolis side are 6 a.m. to midnight and on the St. Paul side from sunrise to sunset. Facilities include biking, hiking, cross-country skiing.

CENTRAL MISSISSIPPI RIVERFRONT   Phone: (612) 661-6800

East and West side of River from Plymouth Ave. Bridge to Portland Ave. in Minneapolis. Hours are 6 a.m. to midnight. Facilities include biking, boat launching, fishing, hiking, picnic areas, power boating.

WIRTH-MEMORIAL PARKWAY   Phone: (612) 661/6800

Victory Memorial Drive provides pathways for walking and biking and an opportunity for pleasure driving between Theodore Wirth Regional Park on the western edge of Minneapolis and Webber Parkway at Irving Ave. North near 45th Ave. in north Minneapolis. Hours are 6 a.m. to midnight. Facilities include biking, hiking, cross-country skiing.

St. Paul's Area Attractions

Minnesota State Capitol—75 Constitution Ave, St Paul, MN 55155 • Beautiful1905 capitol by Cass Gilbert *(architect of the U.S. Supreme Court Bldg)* marble dome is one of largest in the world.

Old Muskego Church—2481 Como Ave, St Paul, MN 55108 • Built by Norwegian immigrants in 1843, moved to current site, Luther Seminary, in 1904; inquire at Information in Campus Center.
Trains at Bandana - Twin City Model Railroad Club—1021 Bandana Blvd E, Bandana Square, St Paul, MN 55108 • 0-scale model railroad layout of the 1930s, 40s & 50s, with landmarks, artifacts.

Minnesota Air Guard Museum—Mpls Air Guard Base MSP IAP, St Paul, MN 55111 • Aircraft, photographs, artifacts tell the history of the Minnesota Air National Guard; A-12 Blackbird.

St. Paul Loop

Trail Length	33.0 miles
Surface	Paved
Uses	Leisure bicycling, in-line skating, jogging
Location & Setting	The "St. Paul Loop" starts in Fort Snelling State Park. Proceed northwest on Minnehaha Ave. through Minnehaha Park. Cross the Ford Bridge to the east bank of the Mississippi River to Hidden Falls Park. The route takes you to the University of Minnesota (St. Paul Campus) through the Minnesota State Fairgrounds to Como Park to Lake Phalen Park. It then follows Johnson Parkway to Indian Mounds Regional Park where you will find excellent views of the Mississippi River and large American Indian Burial Mounds. The Kellog Street Bridge leads into downtown St. Paul.
Information	St. Paul Chamber of Commerce (612) 223-5000
	Emergency Assistance Dial 911
Counties	Ramsey

St. Paul's Area Attractions

Alexander Ramsey House—265 S Exchange St, St Paul, MN 55102 • 1872 home of governor, senator, & sec'y of war Alexander Ramsey; original interior, furnishings; reservations recommended.

Confederate Air Force—Hangar #3, Fleming Field, South St. Paul, MN 55075 • Aviation artifacts, WWII vehicles & aircraft:B-25, PBY-6A, Harvard MkIV and more.

Dakota County Historical Museum—130 3rd Ave N, South St Paul, MN 55075 • Exhibits on county history; research center and cultural events.

Historic Fort Snelling—Hwys 5 and 55, St Paul, MN 55111 • Historic 1820s fort fully restored.

James J. Hill House—240 Summit Ave, St Paul, MN 55102 • Elaborate, 32-room 1891 mansion of James J. Hill; see the art gallery, living quarters, work areas, etc.

Landmark Center #404—75 5th St W, St Paul, MN 55102 • Restored Federal Courts Building, built in 1902, programs include performing and visual arts, civic activities.

Minnesota History Center—345 Kellogg Blvd W, St Paul, MN 55102 • Museum, restaurant, research center in beautiful setting overlooking downtown St. Paul.

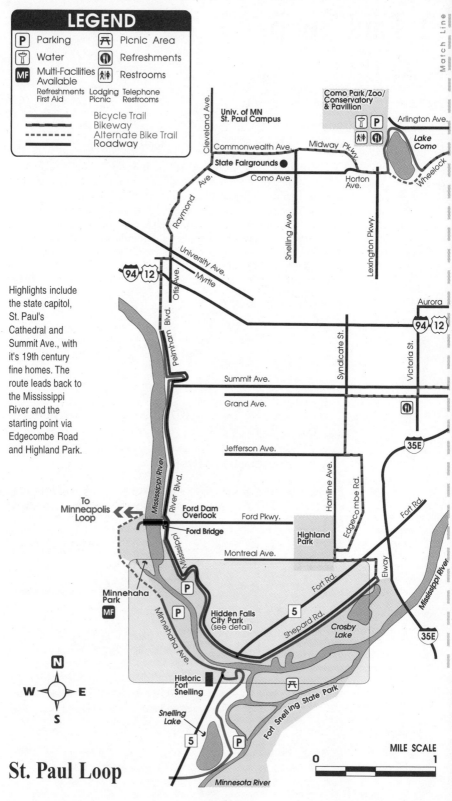

LEGEND

P Parking	**⛩** Picnic Area
🚰 Water	**🍴** Refreshments
MF Multi-Facilities Available	**🚻** Restrooms

Refreshments   Lodging   Telephone
First Aid   Picnic   Restrooms

Bicycle Trail
Bikeway
Alternate Bike Trail
Roadway

Highlights include the state capitol, St. Paul's Cathedral and Summit Ave., with it's 19th century fine homes. The route leads back to the Mississippi River and the starting point via Edgecombe Road and Highland Park.

Como Park/Zoo/ Conservatory & Pavillion

Univ. of MN St. Paul Campus

Cleveland Ave.

Commonwealth Ave.   Midway Pkwy.

Arlington Ave.

Lake Como

State Fairgrounds ●

Como Ave.   Horton Ave.

Wheelock

Raymond Ave.

Snelling Ave.

Lexington Pkwy.

University Ave.

94 **12**

Otis Ave.

Myrtle

Pelham Blvd.

Aurora

94 **12**

Victoria St.

Syndicate St.

Summit Ave.

Grand Ave.

🍴

Jefferson Ave.

35E

Mississippi River

River Blvd.

Hamline Ave.

Edgecombe Rd.

Fort Rd.

To Minneapolis Loop ◄◄←

Ford Dam Overlook

Ford Pkwy.

Highland Park

Ford Bridge

Montreal Ave.

Elway

Minnehaha Park

MF

P

P

Minnehaha Ave.

Hidden Falls City Park (see detail)

5

Fort Rd.

Shepard Rd.

Crosby Lake

Mississippi River

35E

N
W ✦ **E**
S

Historic Fort Snelling

⛩

Fort Snelling State Park

Snelling Lake

5

P

Minnesota River

MILE SCALE
0   1

St. Paul Loop

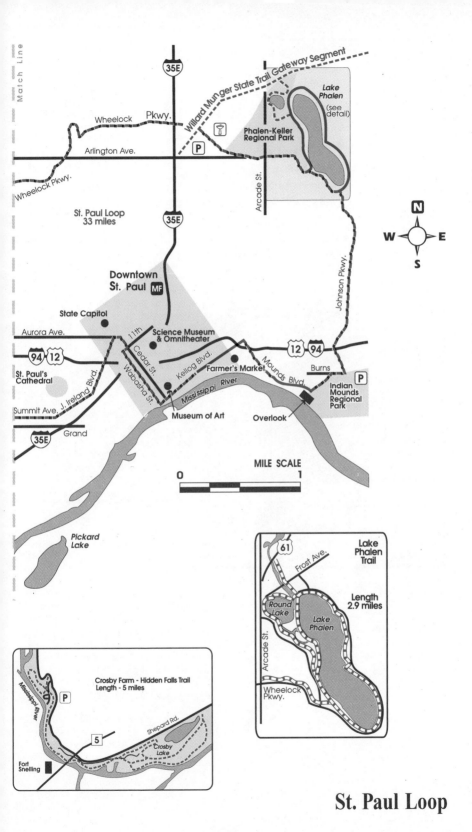

35E

Willard Munger State Trail Gateway Segment

Wheelock Pkwy.

Arlington Ave.

Wheelock Pkwy.

St. Paul Loop
33 miles

35E

Lake
Phalen
(see
detail)

Phalen-Keller
Regional Park

Arcade St.

P

N
W E
S

Downtown
St. Paul MF

State Capitol

Johnson Pkwy.

Aurora Ave.

94 12

St. Paul's
Cathedral

Summit Ave.

35E Grand

11th

Science Museum
& Omnitheater

Cedar St.

Wabasha St.

Kellog Blvd.

J. Ireland Blvd.

Farmer's Market

Mississippi River

Museum of Art

Mounds Blvd.

12 94

Burns

P

Indian
Mounds
Regional
Park

Overlook

MILE SCALE
0   1

Pickard
Lake

61

Frost Ave.

Lake
Phalen
Trail

Round
Lake

Lake
Phalen

Length
2.9 miles

Arcade St.

Wheelock
Pkwy.

Mississippi River

P

5

Shepard Rd.

Crosby Farm - Hidden Falls Trail
Length - 5 miles

Crosby
Lake

Fort
Snelling

St. Paul Loop

Northwest Metro

Minneapolis St. Paul Area

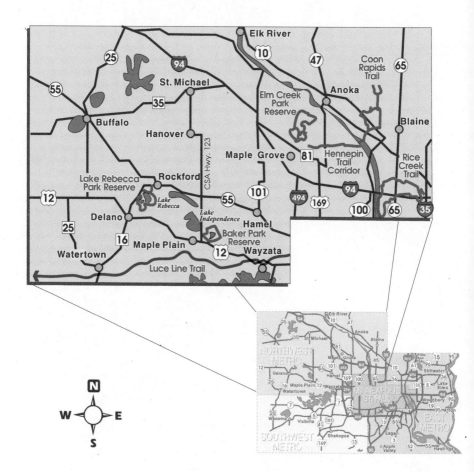

Northwest Metro
LOCAL AREA PARKS

FISH LAKE   (612) 420-3423

Fish Lake Regional Park is located in Maple Grove and offers a variety of outdoor recreational facilities in a beautiful, wooded, lakeside setting. The 160 acre park provides challenging hills for hikers. In-line skate rental is available and skating lessons are offered. There is a parking fee, and normal hours are from 5 a.m. to sunset. Park facilities include biking, boat launching, canoeing, fishing, hiking, ice fishing, picnic areas, power boating and sailing.

COON RAPIDS DAM   (612) 757-4700

This 610 acre Regional Park is located on the Mississippi River between Coon Rapids and Brooklyn Park. Interpretive programs and displays are offered at the West Visitor Center. Bike and in-line skate rental is available. There is also a visitor/interpretive center on the Anoka County side. There is a parking fee, and normal hours are from 5 a.m. to sunset.

Park facilities include biking, boat launching, canoeing, creative play areas, fishing, hiking, ice fishing, nature interpretation, picnic area, power boating, cross-country skiing, snow shoeing.

FRENCH REGIONAL PARK   (612) 559-8891

Located on 310 acres on Medicine Lake in Plymouth. Its Visitor Center offers a concession area and rental equipment for all season - from cross-country skis to volleyballs. There is a parking fee, and normal hours are from 5 a.m. to sunset. Facilities include biking, boat launching, canoeing, creative play areas, fishing, hiking, ice fishing, nature interpretation, picnic area, power boating, sailing, cross-country skiing, snowshoeing.

Northwest Metro Area Attractions

Colonial Hall Museum, home of the Anoka County Historical Society—Colonial Hall, historical exhibits on logging, early Anoka County farming, changing exhibits, educational program, research library, and home of the Anoka County Genealogy Society. Colonial Hall Museum tells the story of its people through county artifacts in a 1904 house. A 1904 house, 17-room home built by husband and wife doctors. Guided tours tell the doctors' story as well as the history of Anoka County. View bison bones, early logging implements, textile and clothing collections and the every day tools. The research library specializes in Anoka County and stores books, microfilm, photos and the archives of the Anoka County Historical Society. Traveling Living History programs feature the Civil War, an 1860's Christmas, and an 1875 Town School Teacher. 1900 3rd Ave S., Anoka, MN 55303, Year round. Tuesday-Friday 12:30-4pm or by appointment, and the first Saturday of each month 12:30-4pm. Adults $2.50; students $1; children 5 & under free, family rate $5. Located on the corner of 3rd & Monroe in Anoka. 1 block S of Main St on 3rd Ave. 1 block from Anoka Co Government Center.

Baker Park Reserve

Trail Length	6.2 miles
Surface	Asphalt
Uses	Leisure bicycling, cross country skiing, in-line skating, jogging
Location & Setting	Located approximately 20 miles west of downtown Minneapolis on County Rd. 19, between Hwy. 12 and 55. Rolling hills, scenic views.
Information	Baker Park Reserve (612) 476-4666 12615 County Road 9 P.O. Box 47320 Plymouth, MN 55447-0320
Counties	Hennepin

LEGEND

P	Parking	🏕	Picnic Area
🏳	Lodging	?	Information
🏠	Shelter	Ⓐ	Camping

—————— Bicycle Trail
- - - - - - Alternate Use Trail
—————— Roadway

To **LORETTO** & Hwy. 55

201

Ⓐ Camp Ihduhapi

19

Hamel Rd.

Spurzem Lake

Halfmoon Lake

201

Lake Independence

2.0 mi.

Ⓐ

Halfmoon Group Camp

Ⓐ

?

24

Parkview Dr.

? P
🏕 Ⓐ

6 mi. Loop

Academy Marsh

Ⓐ Oak Knoll Group Camp

Homestead Trail

Perkins- ville Rd.

19 29

MAPLE PLAIN

P

12

Trumpeter Swan Refuge

Lake Katrina

Katrina Group Ⓐ Camp

201

19

Townline Rd.

Starkey Rd.

12

Trail Access

6

Old Crystal Bay Rd.

Classen Lake

To **LONG LAKE**

N
W   E
S

DIRECTIONS

From Hwy. 12, take County Rd. 29 north to County Rd. 19, and follow 19 north to the main park entrance. From Hwy. 55, take County Rd. 24 west to County Rd. 19, turn south and follow 19 to the main park entrance; or take Hwy. 55 to County Rd. 19, turn south and follow 19 to the main entrance. take Hwy. 55 to County Rd. 19, turn south and follow 19 to the main entrance.

Coon Rapids' Trails

Trail Length	20.0 miles (combination paths and road connectors)
Surface	Paved
Uses	Leisure bicycling, in-line skating, jogging
Location & Setting	To reach Coon Rapids Dam Regional Park, take Coon Rapids Boulevard 2 miles west from the intersection of Highways 10 & 47, then south on Egret Boulevard to the parks entrance. The Bunker Hills Park Reserve is reached by taking Bunker Lake Boulevard west off Highway 65 for about a mile to the parks entrance. Riverfront, urban streets, woods.
Information	Coon Rapids Dam Regional Park (612) 757-4700
Counties	Hennepin

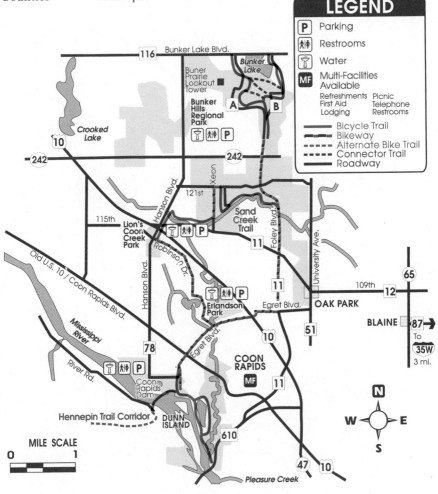

Elm Creek Park Reserve

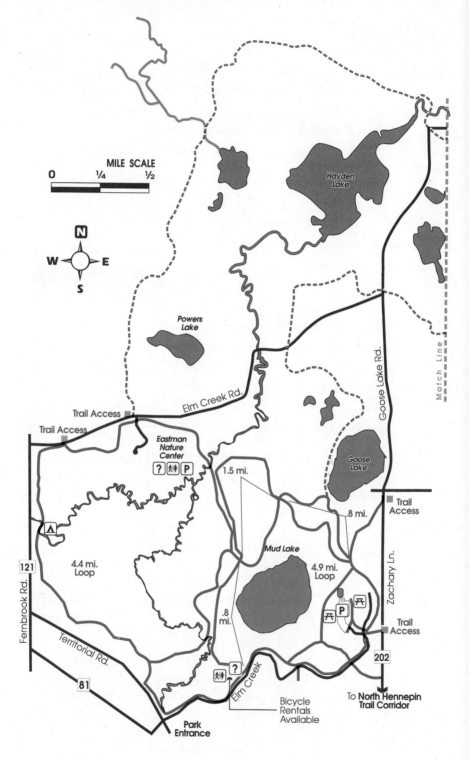

MILE SCALE

0   ¼   ½

N
W — E
S

Hayden Lake

Powers Lake

Match Line

Elm Creek Rd.

Goose Lake Rd.

Trail Access

Trail Access

Eastman Nature Center

? 🚹 P

Goose Lake

1.5 mi.

.8 mi.

Trail Access

🏕

4.4 mi. Loop

Mud Lake

4.9 mi. Loop

Fernbrook Rd.

121

.8 mi.

🏕 P 🏕

Zachary Ln.

Trail Access

Territorial Rd.

81

🚹 ?

Elm Creek

202

Bicycle Rentals Available

To **North Hennepin Trail Corridor**

Park Entrance

Ellingson Car Museum—20950 Rogers Drive, Rogers, MN 55374 • Open year round. Monday-Saturday 10am-6pm; Sunday noon-5pm; closed Thanksgiving, Christmas, New Year's Day, Easter. Over 90 different cars, trucks and motorcycles set up by decade, historic videos and memorabilia accompany each display; displays include WWII tank, rendition of 1950s drive-in movie with old film clips, speed shop, replica of 1960s drag strip. Adults $5; kids (12 and under) free; seniors $4.50. Free parking. Exit Hwy 101 from I-94.

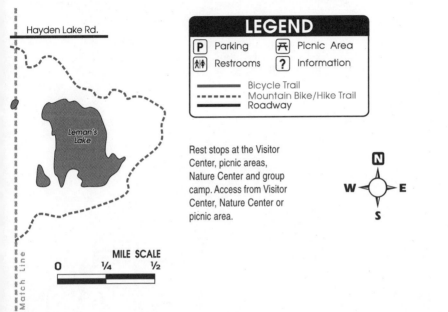

Elm Creek Park Reserve

Trail Length	19.3 miles (10 miles newly constructed)
Surface	Asphalt
Uses	Leisure bicycling, cross country skiing, in-line skating, jogging
Location & Setting	Located northwest of Osseo, between the communities of Champlin, Dayton and Maple Grove. Take County Rd. 81 northwest to Territorial Rd. Turn right and follow to the park entrance. Hilly terrain. Trail connects with North Hennepin Trail Corridor.
Information	Elm Creek Park Reserve 12615 County Road 9 P.O Box 47320 Plymouth, MN 55447-0320 (612) 424-5511
Counties	Hennepin

Hennepin Trail Corridor

Trail Length	7.2 miles
Surface	Asphalt
Uses	Leisure bicycling, in-line skating, jogging
Location & Setting	Connects the Coon Rapids Dam Regional Park to Elm Creek Park Reserve. Coon Rapids Park is located on the Mississippi River in Brooklyn Park. From Highway 252, turn west on County Rd. 30, then take County Rd. 12 north to park entrance. Relatively flat terrain.
Information	Hennepin Park Trail Corridor 12615 County Road 9 Plymouth, MN 55441-1248 (612) 424-8172
Counties	Hennepin

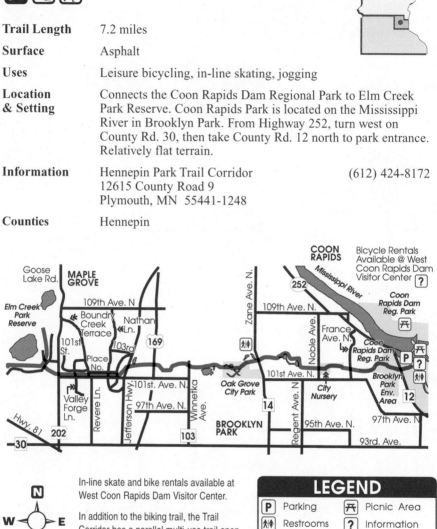

In-line skate and bike rentals available at West Coon Rapids Dam Visitor Center.

In addition to the biking trail, the Trail Corridor has a parallel multi-use trail open to horseback riding, snowmobiling and cross country skiing.

LEGEND

P Parking	🎋 Picnic Area
🚻 Restrooms	**?** Information
——— Bicycle Trail	
——— Roadway	

Nearby Area Attractions

Brooklyn Park Historical Farm—4345 101st Ave N, Brooklyn Park, MN 55443 • May-Aug: Wed. & Sun. noon - 4 pm. Depiction of rural Minnesota at the turn of the century, guided tours of restored farmstead, hands-on activities, living history events in the fall. $.50-$3. Free parking. I-94 North or I-694 to 252, North to 93rd Ave. North (4.1 mi), West to Regent Avenue North (2.1mi), North to 101st Ave North (1mi), East to 4345 101st Ave. North (.5 mi).

Lake Rebecca Park Reserve

🚲 ⛷ 🛼 🚶

Trail Length	6.5 miles
Surface	Asphalt
Uses	Leisure bicycling, cross country skiing, in-line skating, jogging
Location & Setting	Located approximately 30 miles west of Minneapolis on County Road 50. Take Highway 55 west to County Road 50, turn left and follow to the park entrance. Hilly trail through scenic, wooded terrain. Two rest stops; water available in picnic area. Access from recreation/picnic area parking lot.
Information	Lake Rebecca Park Reserve (612) 559-9000
Counties	Hennepin

ROCKFORD

50

Total = 6.8 mi.

55

Crow River

Trumpeter Swan Overlook   .8 mi.

.7 mi.

Bicycle Rentals Available

.5 mi.

P

🏕 Sarah Creek Group Camp

Park Entrance

🏕

Rebecca Rd.

92

Rattail Lake

P

🏕

Deer Woods Trail

Refugee Marsh →→

1.0 mi.

Roy Lake

Lake Rebecca

E. Lake

6.5 mi. Loop

Maintenance Service Rd.

S. Camp Trail

50

Townline Rd.

LEGEND

P	Parking
🏕	Picnic Area
🏕	Camping
—	Bicycle Trail
- - -	Alternate Use Trail
▬	Roadway

1.5 mi.

🏕 South Group Camp

2.3 mi.

11

To DELANO

N W E S

Luce Line State Trail

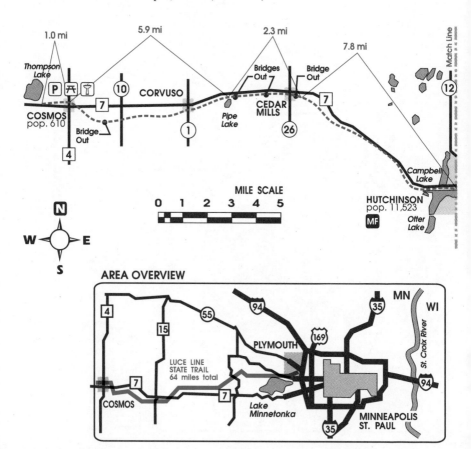

Trail Length	64.0 miles - east segment
Surface	Limestone screenings - east segment Natural groomed - west segment
Uses	Leisure & fat tire bicycling, cross country skiing, snowmobiling, hiking, horseback riding
Location & Setting	The eastern trailhead is located in Plymouth, just west of Minneapolis, and continues for 64 miles to Thompson Lake, west of Cosmos The Luce Line State Trail was developed on an abandoned railroad line. The setting is open country with only scattered tree cover except for woodlands and more urban surroundings near the eastern end.
Information	Luce Line Trail Manager (612) 475-0371 3980 Watertown Road Maple Plain, MN 55359
Counties	Hennepin, Carver, McLeod, Meeker

1.0 mi

5.9 mi

2.3 mi

7.8 mi

Match Line

Thompson Lake

P

COSMOS
pop. 610

Bridge Out

4

7

10

CORVUSO

1

Pipe Lake

Bridges Out

Bridge Out

CEDAR MILLS

26

7

12

Campbell Lake

MILE SCALE

0 1 2 3 4 5

HUTCHINSON
pop. 11,523

MF

Otter Lake

N
W — E
S

AREA OVERVIEW

MN

WI

4

55

94

35

15

169

PLYMOUTH

St. Croix River

LUCE LINE
STATE TRAIL
64 miles total

7

7

COSMOS

Lake Minnetonka

94

35

MINNEAPOLIS
ST. PAUL

HUTCHINSON

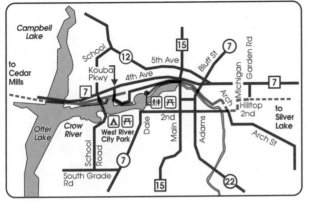

Limestone surface continues to County Rd. 9, 1 mile west of parking area. You can continue to Hutchinson via County Rd. 9 (south) and then west on State HWY 7. The trail continues from HWY 9 on County Route 85 (235th Street). Restaurants, restrooms, picnic, and lodging available.

MILE SCALE

0   1   2   3   4   5

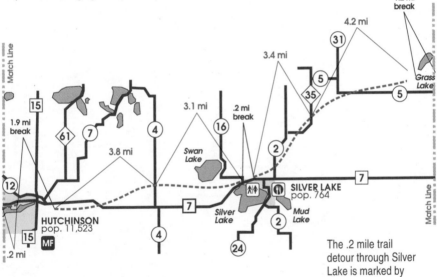

The .2 mile trail detour through Silver Lake is marked by signs. Restrooms, restaurant available in Silver Lake.

Trail detour of 1.9 miles begins just east of Hutchinson and is marked by signs. All normal services are available. West River City Park offers a campground and picnic area.

LEGEND

P	Parking	🏕	Picnic Area
⛺	Camping	🍴	Refreshments
💧	Water	🔧	Bicycle Service
MF	Multi-Facilities Available	🚻	Restrooms

Refreshments   Lodging   Telephone
First Aid   Picnic   Restrooms

Bicycle Trail
Bikeway
Alternate Bike Trail
Roadway

Luce Line State Trail

ROUTE SLIP	INCREMENT	TOTAL	ELEV.
Plymouth			1000
Vicksburg Ln.	1.1	1.1	
Old Long Lake Rd.	2.9	4.0	
Orono (Willow Dr.)	2.5	6.5	
Stubbs Bay	1.3	7.8	935
County Rd. 110	2.4	10.2	
Lyndale	3.4	13.6	
HWY 127	2.5	16.1	
Watertown (HWY 10)	3.5	19.6	960
HWY 21	4.5	24.1	
HWY 33	2.0	26.1	
Winsted	3.4	29.5	1010
Trail Break	*1.4*		
HWY 35	4.2	33.7	
Silver Lake (HWY 2)	3.4	37.1	1050
HWY 4	3.1	40.2	
Hutchinson	3.8	44.0	1056
Trail Break	*1.9*		
Cedar Mills	8.0	52.0	
Pipe Lake	2.3	54.3	
Cosmos	5.9	60.2	1112
Thompson Lake	1.0	61.2	

Parking, restrooms, and restaurants near the Watertown trailheads.

WATERTOWN

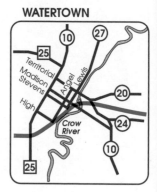

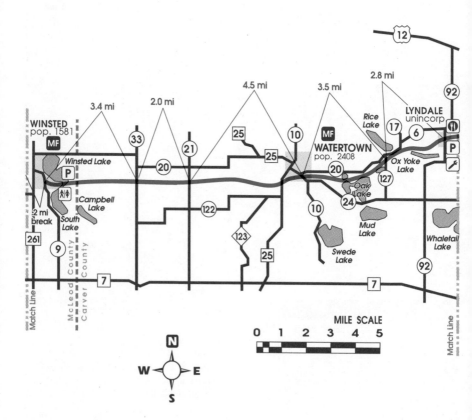

Luce Line State Trail

LEGEND

P	Parking	🌲	Picnic Area
A	Camping	🅜	Refreshments
🚰	Water	🔧	Bicycle Service
MF	Multi-Facilities Available	🚹🚺	Restrooms

Refreshments First Aid / Lodging Picnic / Telephone Restrooms

Bicycle Trail
Bikeway
Alternate Bike Trail
Roadway

East Trailhead

From I-494 exit west on HWY 12 (Wayzata Blvd.) to County Rd. 15 (Gleason Lake Rd.) Turn north and exit to the north on Vicksburg Lane. Continue north to 10th Ave. N. (note sign) and turn west a half block to the parking lot. Restrooms and picnic area available. If you are traveling west on HWY 55, west of I-494, turn south on Vicksburg Lane.

PLYMOUTH TRAILHEAD

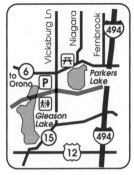

The city of Plymouth has a 1.1 mile paved spur west to I-494.

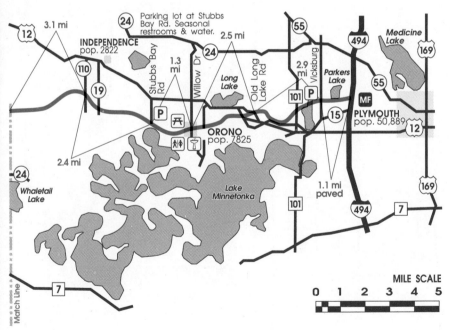

Luce Line State Trail

Rice Creek West Regional Trail
Long Lake Regional Park
Anoka County Riverfront Park

Trail Length	8.0 miles (18.0 miles loop with street routes)
Surface	Paved, gravel
Uses	Leisure bicycling, cross country skiing, in-line skating, jogging
Location & Setting	This path takes you from Long Lake in New Brighton west along Rice Creek through Findley and a ride along the Mississippi River through Anoka County Riverfront Park to 42nd Avenue. From the intersection of I-35W and I-694, take I-35W to Highway 96, then west to 1st Avenue, then south to the park entrance. Waterviews, parkways, urban.
Information	Long Lake Regional Park (612) 777-1707
Counties	Anoka, Ramsey

LEGEND

P	Parking	🏕	Picnic Area
🚰	Water	🚻	Restrooms

Bicycle Trail
Bikeway
Alternate Bike Trail
Roadway

The route is mainly level except for some short grades and gravel paths along Rice Creek east of Central. There is a short road connection on Stinson, and another stretch with a wide bike lane along East River Rd. Use care in crossing major streets. The path takes you under the Hwy. I-694. Long Lake Park's facilities include a swimming beach, bath house, picnic and play areas.

Southwest Metro

Minneapolis
St. Paul Area

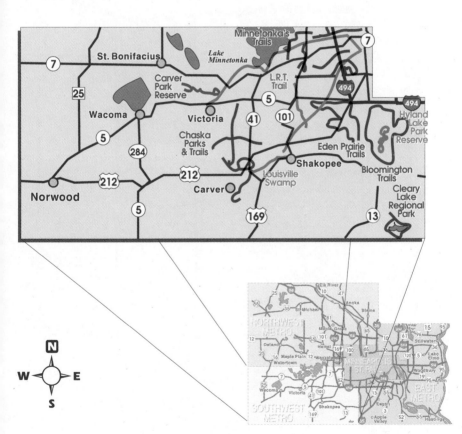

Bloomington Trails

Trail Length	19.0 miles
Surface	Paved
Uses	Leisure bicycling, in-line skating, jogging
Location & Setting	Bloomington is a suburb located southwest of the Twin Cities. A convenient starting point is from the main parking lot in Hyland Lake Park Reserve. Take Normandale Blvd. south from I-494 to 84th Street. Turn west and follow 84th to East Bush Lake Road, then south to the entrance. Be prepared for hills. Park & suburban setting.
Information	Hyland Lake Park Reserve (612) 941-4362
Counties	Hennepin

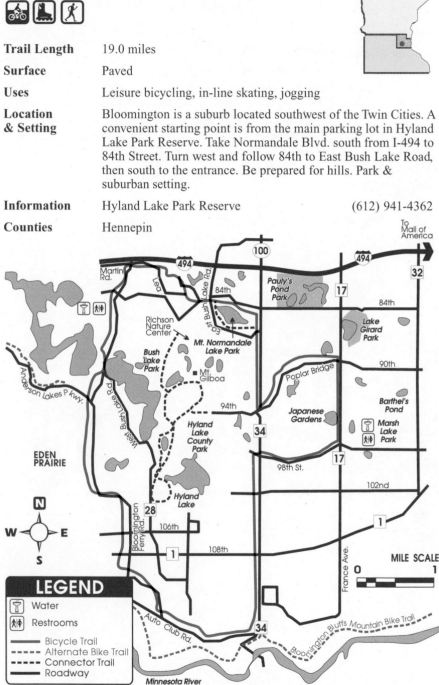

Bloomington is the third largest city in Minnesota and the home of "Mall of America". Among the sites along the route is the Normandale Japanese Garden, which was exquisitely designed by Takao Watanabe, a landscape artist from Tokyo, and Richardson Nature Center, with its many nature attractions.

Carver Park Reserve
Hennepin Parks

Trail Length	8.5 miles
Surface	Asphalt
Uses	Leisure bicycling, cross country skiing, in-line skating, jogging
Location & Setting	Located in Victoria, on Carver County Road 11. Take Highway 7 west from Minneapolis and turn left on County Road 11 or take Highway 5 west from Minneapolis and turn right on County Road 11. Follow signs to picnic area or trailhead. Moderate terrain. Rest stops at Lowry Nature Center and Parley Lake picnic area. Access from Nature Center or picnic area.
Information	' Carver Park Reserve (612) 472-4911 12615 County Road P.O. Box 47320 Plymouth, MN 55447-0320
Counties	Carver

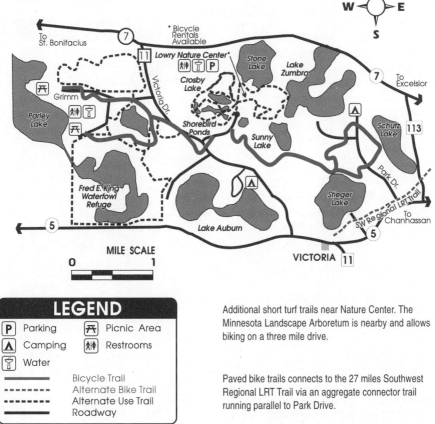

LEGEND

P	Parking	**⛱**	Picnic Area
A	Camping	**⚥**	Restrooms
Water			

—— Bicycle Trail
------ Alternate Bike Trail
— — Alternate Use Trail
—— Roadway

Additional short turf trails near Nature Center. The Minnesota Landscape Arboretum is nearby and allows biking on a three mile drive.

Paved bike trails connects to the 27 miles Southwest Regional LRT Trail via an aggregate connector trail running parallel to Park Drive.

Chaska's Trails

Trail Length	17.0 miles
Surface	Paved, gravel*
Uses	Leisure bicycling, cross country skiing, in-line skating, hiking
Location & Setting	Chaska is located in Carver County, southwest of the Twin Cities. The City Square is a good place to start, but there are numerous access points with parking along the route. You'll travel past lakes, through wooded ravines, experiencing some hills in addition to suburban areas.
Information	City of Chaska (612) 448-2851
Counties	Carver

Nearby Area Attractions

Lowry Nature Center—Box 270, Victoria, MN 55386 • Open year round. Tues.-Sat. 9am-5pm, Sun noon-5pm; also open Memorial Day-Labor Day: Mon 9am-5pm. This park has 4 large lakes, camping, canoeing, hiking, biking and horseback riding trails, recreation play area, bird feeding station, 4 observation decks and a half-mile floating dock in the marsh. Also, beehive observation, family programs and bike rental. Informational displays, self guided trail brochures. Hennepin park permit required. Annual: $20; Daily: $4. Free parking available the first Tues. of each month. Located 8.5 mi W of Excelsior on Co Rd 11. Also 6 mi W of Chanhassen on Hwy 5, then 1.5 mi N on CR 11.

Scott County Historical Society—235 S Fuller St, Shakopee, MN 55379 • Open year round. Wed-Sat 10am-4pm. This museum contains African art and artifacts as well as local history. Donations appreciated. Free parking. 1 blk N of Court House in Shakopee.

Historic Murphy's Landing—2187 East Hwy 101, Shakopee, MN 55379 • Mar-Dec. Memorial Day-Labor Day: T-Sun 10am-5pm; Mar-Dec: M-F by reservation; Thanksgiving-Christmas: Sat & Sun 10am-4pm. Living history re-creation of 1840-90 settler life; fur trader cabin, farms, blacksmith, town square, shops; boat excursion, schoolhouse classes, costumed interpreters, horse drawn trolley, restau-

* The path between Chaska City Square and Shakopee is paved. The route along Pioneer Trail Road is a paved shoulder. The remainder of the route is mostly gravel.

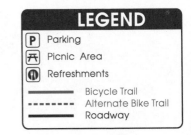

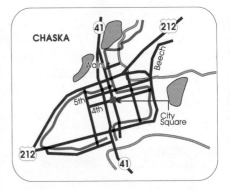

rant, gift shop; located on 87 acres in the Minnesota River Valley. Adults $7; seniors & students $6; children (ages 5 & under) free. Group rates (25 or more) are available. Free parking. Located 1 mi E of Shakopee on Hwy 101.

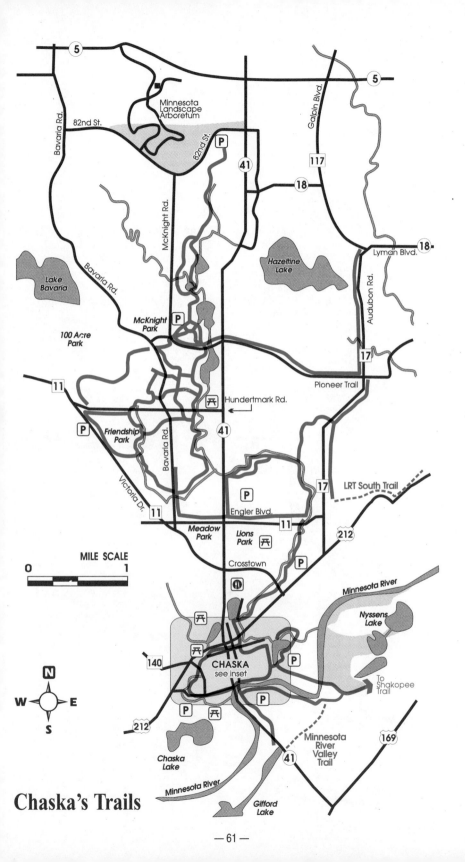

Chaska's Trails

Cleary Lake Regional Park

Trail Length	3.5 miles
Surface	Asphalt
Uses	Leisure bicycling, cross country skiing, in-line skating, jogging
Location & Setting	Near Prior Lake on Scott County Road 27. From Highway 35W, go west on County Road 42, then south on County Road 27, or take I-494 to County Road 18, go south on 18, then east on Highway 101, south on Highway 13, east on County Road 42, then south again on County Road 27 to the park entrance. Flat terrain around the lake with one gradual hill. Three rest stops and one water pump stop. Access at Visitor Center.
Information	Cleary Lake Regional Park (612) 447-2171 12615 County Road 9, P.O. Box 47320 Plymouth, MN 55447-0320
Counties	Scott

In-line skate rentals available.

LEGEND

P Parking	**🎋** Picnic Area
Water	**?** Information
Shelter	**A** Camping
———	Bicycle Trail
- - - - -	Hiking Trail
———	Roadway

To Prior Lake

12

87

Revere Way

Cleary Lake

3.5 mi. Loop

27

Cleary Island

Rest Area

Cleary Point Group Camp

Norway Ridge Group Camp

Basswood Group Camp

Boat Rental Available

Park Entrance

Red Pine Group Camp

Birchwood Group Camp

? Visitor Center

N
W E
S

MILE SCALE
0   ¼   ½

68   190th St.   12

Eden Prairie Trails

Trail Length	20.0 miles
Surface	Paved
Uses	Leisure bicycling, in-line skating, hiking/jogging
Location & Setting	Eden Prairie, a suburb located southwest of the twin cities. The path meanders through the community, looping Staring Lake and Round Lake in route. The city got its name in 1853 from a eastern journalist, Mrs. Elizabeth Ellet, who described the area as a "garden of Eden". A good starting point is the parking lot on the south side of Staring Lake and across from the Planes of Fame Air Museum. Parks, suburban setting.
Information	Eden Prairie City Offices (612) 949-8300 8080 Mitchell Road Eden Prairie, MN 55344-2230
Counties	Hennepin

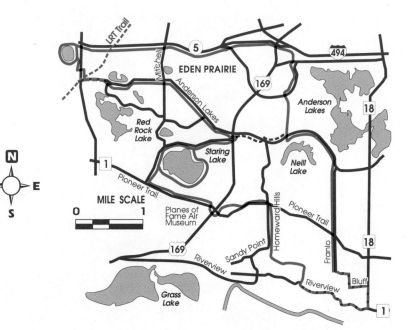

The Planes of Fame Air Museum is well worth the visit. It features restored planes from World War II. It's open Tuesday through Sunday and there is a charge. You can even sign up for a open cockpit flight in a Stearman.

Staring Lake Park — Provides a 2.5 mile bike path around the lake, and a 500 seat amphitheater for concerts and plays throughout the summer.

Hyland Lake Park Reserve

Trail Length 5.5 miles

Surface Asphalt

Uses Leisure bicycling, cross country skiing, in-line skating, jogging

Location & Setting Located on East Bush Lake Road in Bloomington. From I-494, go south on Normandale Boulevard to 84th Street. Turn Right and follow 84th Street to East Bush Lake Road. Go south on East Lake Bush Road and follow the signs to Richard-son Nature Center and Hyland Lake Visitor Center. Northern loop through rolling hills and scenic meadows; southern loop through woodlands. Trails connect to adjacent neighborhoods. Two rest areas. Access from Visitor Center.

Information Hyland Lake Park Reserve
(612) 941-4362
12615 County Road 9
P.O. Box 47320
Plymouth, MN
55447-0320

Counties Hennepin

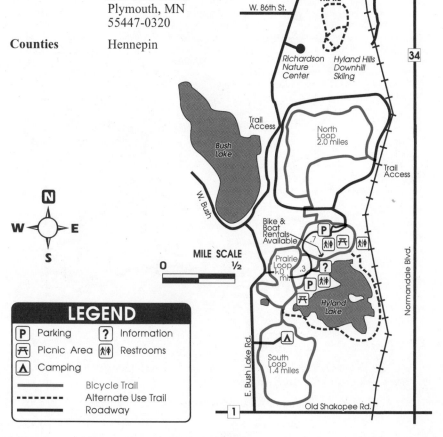

MILE SCALE

0   ½

LEGEND

P Parking **?** Information
A Picnic Area **††** Restrooms
A Camping

——— Bicycle Trail
- - - - Alternate Use Trail
——— Roadway

Louisville Swamp
Minnesota Valley State Recreation Area

Trail Length	4.0 miles
Surface	Paved (plus 13.5 miles grass & dirt trail)
Uses	Leisure bicycling, in-line skating, cross country skiing, hiking
Location & Setting	Southwest of Minneapolis with trailheads in Shakopee and Chaska. There is parking in Chaska off State Highway 41 and in Shakopee at the Huber Park trailhead near city hall, one block east of Highway 169. The trail was built on an old railroad bed. It crosses the Minnesota River on the original railroad swing bridge.
Information	Minnesota Valley State Park (612) 492-6400 19825 Park Boulevard Horden, MN 55352
Counties	Carver

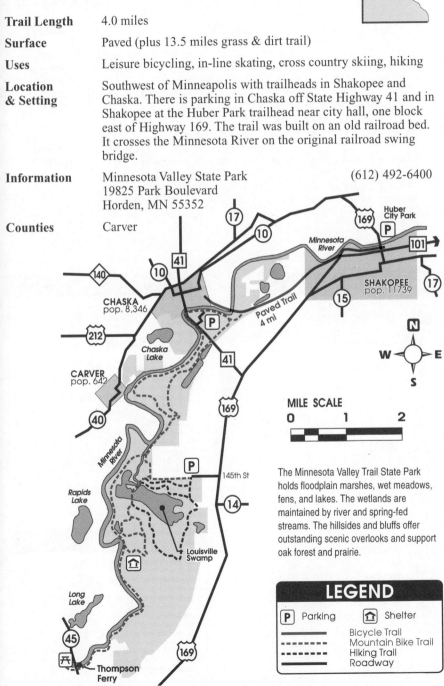

The Minnesota Valley Trail State Park holds floodplain marshes, wet meadows, fens, and lakes. The wetlands are maintained by river and spring-fed streams. The hillsides and bluffs offer outstanding scenic overlooks and support oak forest and prairie.

LEGEND

P Parking	**⌂** Shelter

Bicycle Trail
Mountain Bike Trail
Hiking Trail
Roadway

MILE SCALE
0   1   2

Southwest Metro   LOCAL AREA PARKS

BRYANT LAKE   (612) 941-4518

Located in Eden Prairie, the 170 acre park, nestled among rolling hills is a perfect spot for a summer afternoon outing. There is a parking fee, and normal hours are from 5 a.m. to sunset. Facilities include biking, boat launching, canoeing, fishing, hiking, ice fishing, picnic area, power boating, sailing.

HYLAND LAKE PARK RESERVE   (612) 948-8877

This 1,000 acre park is surrounded by the City of Bloomington. This popular park annually attracts some 450,000 visitors to its nature programs and extensive recreation facilities. Reservation picnic area and group camp sites are available. There is a parking fee and normal hours are 5 a.m. to sunset. Facilities include biking, boat launching, canoeing, creative play area, fishing, golf, hiking, picnic area, sailing, cross-country skiing, snowmobiling, snowshoeing.

MURPHY-HANREHAN PARK RESERVE   (612) 447-6913

The glacial ridges and hilly terrain of northwest Scott County make this 2,400 acre park popular with mountain bikers and hikers, and a challenging cross-country ski area. There is a parking fee and normal hours are from 5 a.m. to sunset. Facilities include mountain biking, hiking, horseback riding, cross-country skiing, snowmobiling.

FACILITIES

- Bicycle Service
- Camping
- First Aid
- Info
- Lodging
- Parking
- Picnic
- Refreshments
- Restrooms
- Shelter
- Water
- MF Multi Facilities Available

Refreshments   First Aid
Telephone   Picnic
Restrooms   Lodging

TRAIL USES

- Mountain Biking
- Leisure Biking
- In Line Skating
- (X-C) Cross-Country Skiing
- Hiking
- Horseback Riding
- Snowmobiling

ROUTES

- Biking Trail
- Bikeway
- Alternate Bike Trail
- Undeveloped Trail
- Alternate Use Trail
- Planned Trail
- Roadway

LRT Trail

Trail Length	North corridor - 15.5 miles South corridor - 11.5 miles
Surface	Crushed limestone - 10 feet wide
Uses	Leisure bicycling, cross country skiing, hiking
Location & Setting	The Southwest Regional LRT Trail includes two corridors that follow abandoned railroad right-of-way through the southwestern metro Twin Cities area. The north corridor begins in Hopkins on the west side of Eighth Avenue North, just north of Main street and runs to downtown Victoria. The south corridor also begins in Hopkins, at the *Park and Ride* lot southeast of the intersection of Eight Avenue South and County Road 3 and extends to Chanhassen.
Information	Hennepin Parks (612) 559-9000 12615 County Road 9 P.O. Box 47320 Plymouth, MN 55447-0320 Trail Hotline (612) 559-6778
Counties	Hennepin, Carver

(See map on following pages)

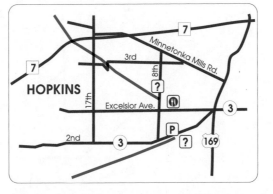

The Trails is two-way and includes wooden bridges and several road crossings. Designated parking areas are available along both corridors. Trail hours are from 5 a.m. to sunset. Motorized vehicles are prohibited.

The Hennepin Parks system consists of 25,000 acres of park land including seven large park reserves, five regional park Noerenberg Gardens, the North Hennepin Regional Trail Corridor besides the LRT trail.

The average trail grade is 1%, with a maximum of 5%. The average cross slope is 0% with a maximum of 1%.

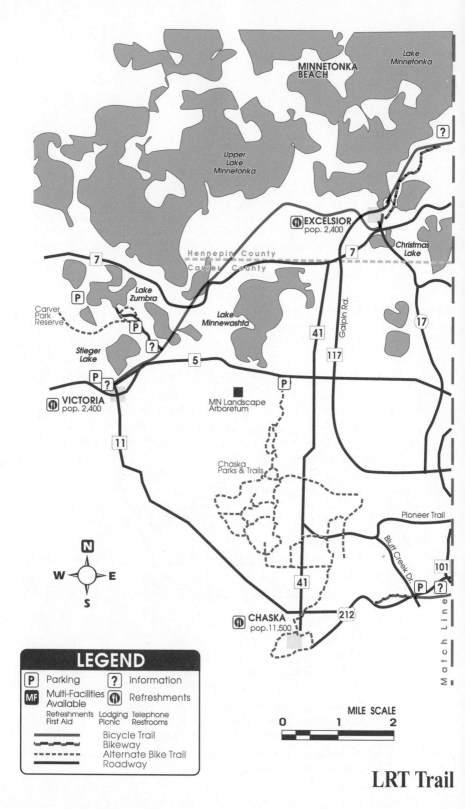

LRT Trail

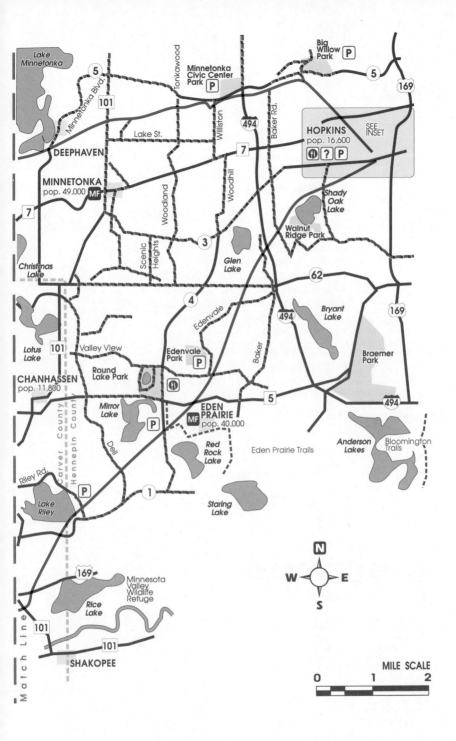

LRT Trail

Minnetonka's Trails

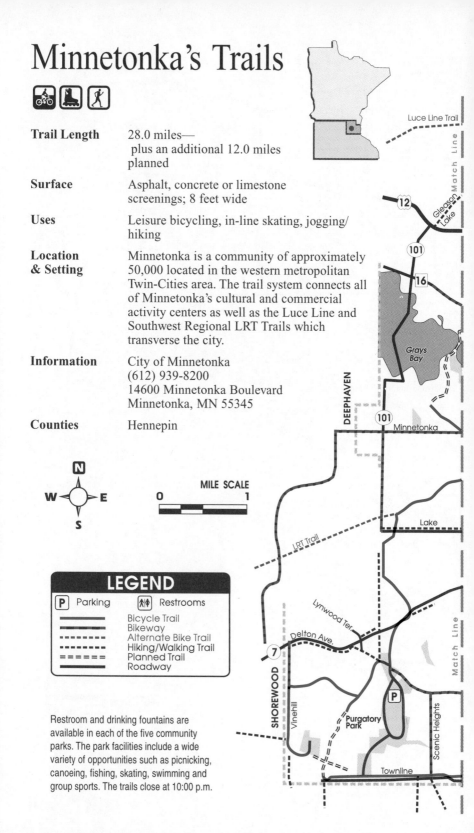

Trail Length 28.0 miles—
plus an additional 12.0 miles
planned

Surface Asphalt, concrete or limestone
screenings; 8 feet wide

Uses Leisure bicycling, in-line skating, jogging/
hiking

**Location
& Setting** Minnetonka is a community of approximately
50,000 located in the western metropolitan
Twin-Cities area. The trail system connects all
of Minnetonka's cultural and commercial
activity centers as well as the Luce Line and
Southwest Regional LRT Trails which
transverse the city.

Information City of Minnetonka
(612) 939-8200
14600 Minnetonka Boulevard
Minnetonka, MN 55345

Counties Hennepin

LEGEND

| P | Parking | 🚹🚺 | Restrooms |

Bicycle Trail
Bikeway
Alternate Bike Trail
Hiking/Walking Trail
Planned Trail
Roadway

Restroom and drinking fountains are
available in each of the five community
parks. The park facilities include a wide
variety of opportunities such as picnicking,
canoeing, fishing, skating, swimming and
group sports. The trails close at 10:00 p.m.

At most uncontrolled intersections with major roadways, the trail crosses the road in a pedestrian underpass or overpass. The trail system is plowed during the winter months, making it available throughout the year. Cross country skiing and snowmobiling are prohibited.

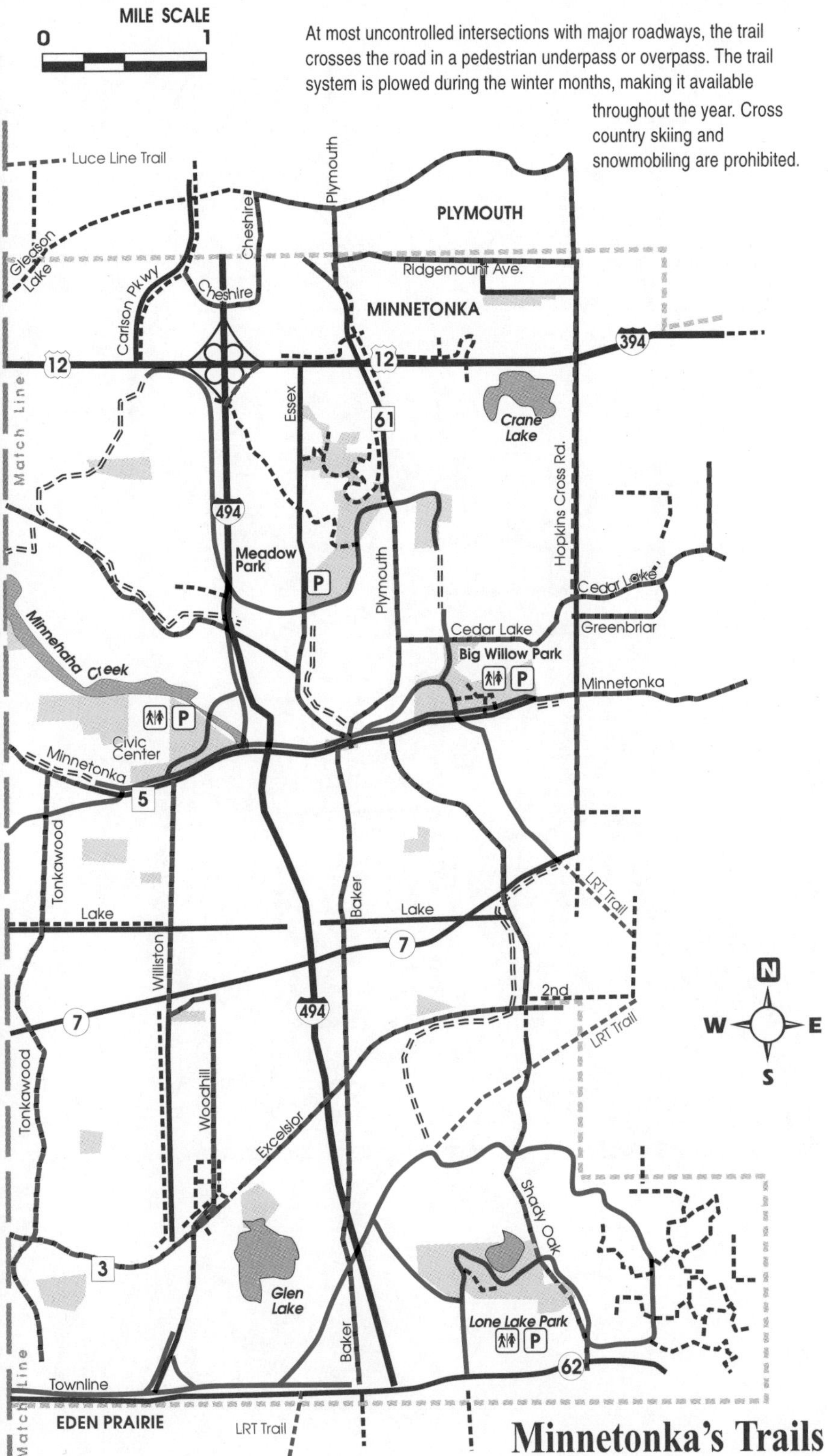

Luce Line Trail

Gleason Lake

Cheshire

Plymouth

PLYMOUTH

Carlson Pkwy

Cheshire

Ridgemount Ave.

MINNETONKA

Match Line

12

12

394

Essex

61

Crane Lake

494

Meadow Park

P

Plymouth

Hopkins Cross Rd.

Cedar Lake

Minnehaha Creek

Cedar Lake

Greenbriar

Big Willow Park

P

Minnetonka

Civic Center

P

Minnetonka

5

Tonkawood

Lake

Williston

Baker

Lake

7

LRT Trail

2nd

7

LRT Trail

N
W E
S

Tonkawood

Woodhill

494

Excelsior

Shady Oak

3

Glen Lake

Baker

Lone Lake Park

P

62

Townline

EDEN PRAIRIE

LRT Trail

Match Line

Minnetonka's Trails

East Metro

Minneapolis
St. Paul Area

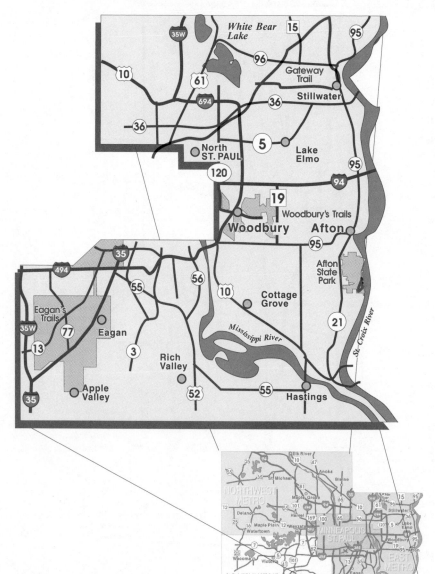

Afton State Park

Trail Length	4.0 miles
Surface	Asphalt .... 3.0 miles
	Crushed limestone .... 1.0 mile
Uses	Leisure bicycling, cross country skiing, hiking
Location & Setting	Located less than an hour from the Twin Cities in Washington County. The park entrance is off Highway 20, just east of Highway 21. Afton State Park lies on the bluffs overlooking the St. Croix River where it is cut by deep ravines. Outcrops of sandstone jut from the side of the ravines. The rugged terrain affords spectacular view of the St. Croix Valley. Above the forested ravines are rolling fields and pastures.
Information	Afton State Park Manager (612) 436-5391
	6959 Peller Avenue South
	Hastings, MN 55033
Counties	Washington

LEGEND

P	Parking	🎎	Picnic Area
🏠	Shelter	?	Information
🚰	Water	🚻	Restrooms
🏕	Camping		Overlooks ■

—————— Bicycle Trail
- - - - - - - Alternate Use Trail
—————— Roadway

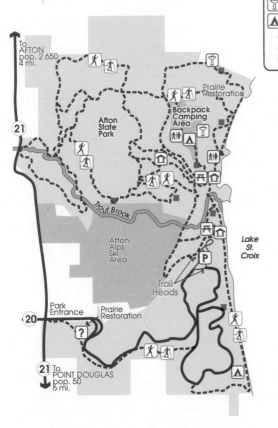

Afton State Park was established in 1969. The park offer opportunities for biking, hiking, cross country skiing, swimming, picnicking and camping. Wildlife includes fox, deer, badgers, hawks, eagles and warblers. In addition to biking, there are 18.0 miles of hiking and cross country ski trails and 5 miles of horseback riding trails. The Visitor Center facilities include interpretive, information and a pay telephone. The camp is closed from 10 pm to 8 am except for campers.

MILE SCALE

0 _____ 1

Eagan's Trails

Trail Length	Over 50.0 miles
Surface	Paved
Uses	Leisure bicycling, in-line skating, jogging
Location & Setting	The city of Eagan, southeast of the Twin Cities. The routes includes connections between Fort Snelling State Park, the Zoo, Lebanon Hills Regional Park and the Minnesota Valley Visitor Center. While the routes are mostly off-road, many are hilly.
Information	Fort Snelling State Park (612) 725-2390
	Minnesota Valley Visitor Center (612) 335-2323
	Patrick Eagan Park (612) 681-4660
Counties	Dakota

LEGEND

P	Parking	**🍴**	Refreshments
Ⓣ	Water	**?**	Information
MF	Multi-Facilities Available	**👥**	Restrooms
	Refreshments First Aid	Lodging Picnic	Telephone Restrooms

———— Bicycle Trail
———— Bikeway
-------- Alternate Bike Trail
———— Roadway

Dakota County Parks

Spring Lake Park Reserve
Phone: (612) 437-6608
Hiking, cross countryskiing & scenic trails
wind through woods and along the bluffs high above the Mississippi River. Park visitors will enjoy activities such as a model airplane flying field and archery trail. Facilities include: a heated lodge, an outdoor classroom and a large open playfield with a sand volleyball court. South of Twin Cities on Hwy 55 to CR 42, east 2 mi. 8am to 11pm.

Lake Byllesby Regional Park
Phone: (612) 437-6608
Camping, canoeing, hiking and sailing are just a few of the activities you can enjoy at Lake Byllesby Regional Park. Nestled in the Cannon Valley along the shore of Lake Byllesby Reservoir, the park offers many acres of woods and open area and a large beautiful lake. South of Twin Cities on Hwy 52 to CR86 (near Cannon Falls). West on CR 86, immediate left on Harry Ave, south 1.5 mi. 5am to 11pm.

Lebanon Hills
Phone: (612) 437-6608
Activities such as biking, camping, canoeing, hiking, nature interpretation, cross country skiing and snowshoeing are available to visitors of Lebanon Hills Regional Park, which consists of over 2,000 acres of lakes, hills and woods, and a beautiful swimming beach. See the map inset of the park for mountain biking or hiking alternatives. The mountain biking trail is hilly and located in deep hardwoods. Its surface is dirt and grass. 5am to 11pm, swim beach open 11am to 8pm.

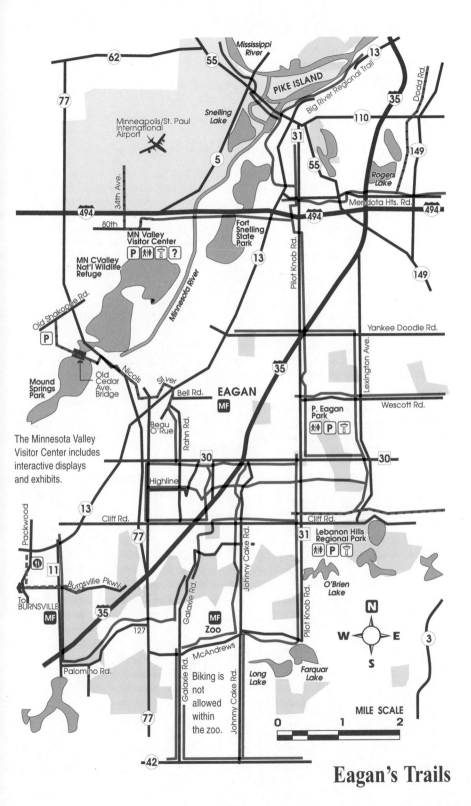

The Minnesota Valley Visitor Center includes interactive displays and exhibits.

Biking is not allowed within the zoo.

MILE SCALE
0   1   2

Eagan's Trails

Gateway Trail

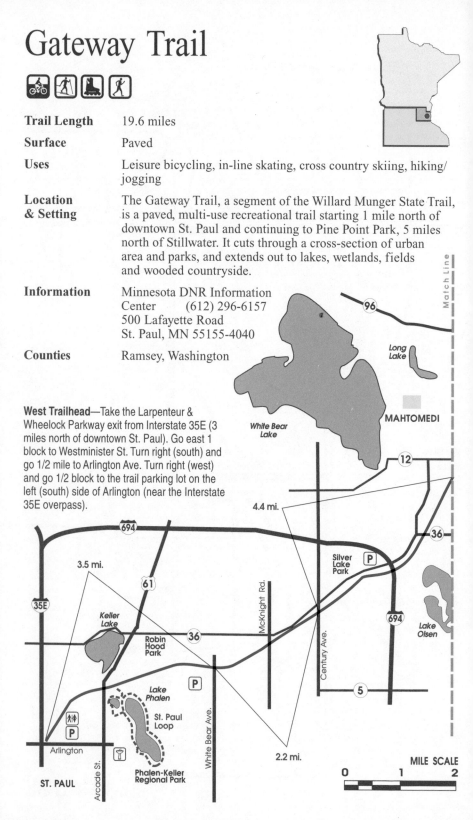

Trail Length 19.6 miles

Surface Paved

Uses Leisure bicycling, in-line skating, cross country skiing, hiking/jogging

Location & Setting The Gateway Trail, a segment of the Willard Munger State Trail, is a paved, multi-use recreational trail starting 1 mile north of downtown St. Paul and continuing to Pine Point Park, 5 miles north of Stillwater. It cuts through a cross-section of urban area and parks, and extends out to lakes, wetlands, fields and wooded countryside.

Information Minnesota DNR Information Center   (612) 296-6157
500 Lafayette Road
St. Paul, MN 55155-4040

Counties Ramsey, Washington

West Trailhead—Take the Larpenteur & Wheelock Parkway exit from Interstate 35E (3 miles north of downtown St. Paul). Go east 1 block to Westminister St. Turn right (south) and go 1/2 mile to Arlington Ave. Turn right (west) and go 1/2 block to the trail parking lot on the left (south) side of Arlington (near the Interstate 35E overpass).

Match Line

96

Long Lake

MAHTOMEDI

White Bear Lake

12

4.4 mi.

36

694

Silver Lake Park P

3.5 mi.

61

35E

Keller Lake

36

Robin Hood Park

McKnight Rd.

694

Lake Olsen

P

Lake Phalen

St. Paul Loop

Century Ave.

5

2.2 mi.

White Bear Ave.

P

Arlington

Arcade St.

Phalen-Keller Regional Park

ST. PAUL

MILE SCALE

0   1   2

MILE SCALE

0 1 2

120th St. N.

Pine Point County Park

CARNELIAN JUNCTION

4.5 mi.

15

55

Silver Lake

Manning Ave.

Match Line

96

P

DULUTH JUNCTION

96

Norell Ave.

Pioneer Park

Owens

12

Kears

2.3 mi.

Laurel

STILLWATER

36

Lake De Montreville Park

Lake Jane

East Trailhead—Near Pine Point Park, 5 miles north of Stillwater on County Rd. 55. There is a small fee for parking.

Between Interstate 694 underpass and the east trailhead near Pine Point Park (9.7 miles) is a dual trailway: unpaved, for horseback riding and paved for X-C skiing.

LEGEND

P	Parking	🏕	Picnic Area
🚹🚺	Restrooms	🚰	Water

Bicycle Trail
Bikeway
Alternate Bike Trail
Roadway

Gateway Trail

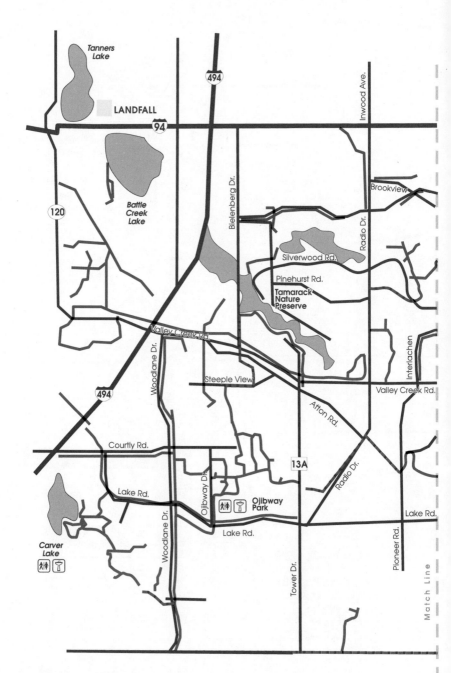

Woodbury's Trails

Woodbury's Trails

Trail Length	35.0+ miles
Surface	Paved

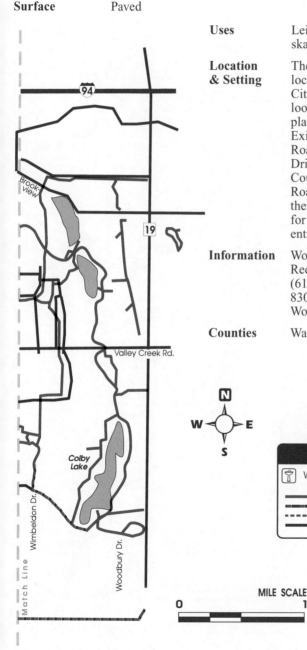

Uses	Leisure bicycling, in-line skating, hiking/jogging
Location & Setting	The city of Woodbury is located southeast of the Twin Cities. The route forms a large loop through the city. A good place to start is Ojibway Park. Exit I-494 on Valley Creek Road. Head east to Woodlane Drive and then south to Courtly Road. East on Courtly Road to Ojibway Drive and then south on Ojibway Drive for one block to the park entrance.
Information	Woodbury Parks & Recreation Department (612) 739-5972 8301 Valley Creek Road Woodbury, MN 55125
Counties	Washington

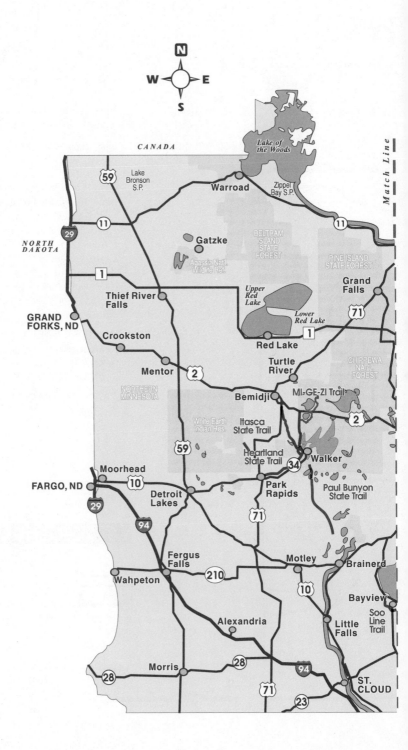

N
W E
S

CANADA

Match Line

Lake of
the Woods

59

Lake
Bronson
S.P.

Warroad

Zippel
Bay S.P.

11

29

11

NORTH
DAKOTA

Gatzke

BELTRAMI
ISLAND
STATE
FOREST

PINE ISLAND
STATE FOREST

1

Agassiz Natl.
Wildlife Ref.

Upper
Red
Lake

Grand
Falls

Thief River
Falls

71

GRAND
FORKS, ND

Crookston

Lower
Red Lake

1

Red Lake

Mentor

2

Turtle
River

CHIPPEWA
NATL
FOREST

NORTHERN
MINNESOTA

Bemidji

MI-GE-ZI Trail

White Earth
Indian Res.

Itasca
State Trail

2

59

Heartland
State Trail

34

Walker

Moorhead

10

Park
Rapids

Paul Bunyon
State Trail

FARGO, ND

29

Detroit
Lakes

71

94

Fergus
Falls

Motley

Brainerd

Wahpeton

210

10

Bayview

Alexandria

Little
Falls

Soo
Line
Trail

Morris

28

28

94

ST.
CLOUD

71

23

— 80 —

Northern Minnesota

Heartland State Trail

Trail Length	50.0 miles
Surface	Asphalt, natural-groomed
Uses	Leisure bicycling, cross-country skiing, in-line skating, snowmobiling, hiking
Location & Setting	The Heartland Trail is a 50 mile multiple-use state trail constructed on an abandoned railroad line. The Trail has two segments. The East-West segment is 28 miles long and asphalt paved, running between Park Rapids Walker. The North-South segment is 22 miles long, undeveloped but mowed, and runs between Walker and just south of Cass Lake. The East West segment is mostly open area while the North-South segment is wooded and lakes.
Information	Heartland Trail Headquarters (218) 652-4054 P.O. Box 112 Nevis, MN 56467
Counties	Hubbard, Cass

West Trailhead—Begins in Heartland Park in Park Rapids. Going east on HWY 34 through Park Rapids, you turn north on Central Avenue (there is a sign). Turn west on North Street which leads into the park which offers excellent facilities.

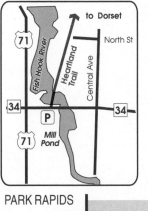

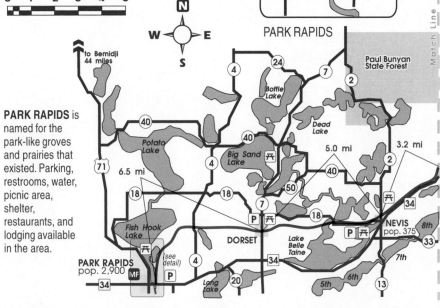

PARK RAPIDS is named for the park-like groves and prairies that existed. Parking, restrooms, water, picnic area, shelter, restaurants, and lodging available in the area.

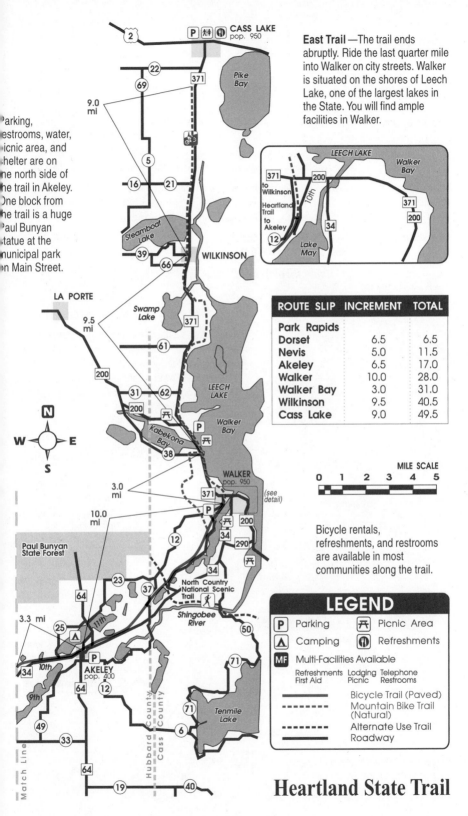

East Trail —The trail ends abruptly. Ride the last quarter mile into Walker on city streets. Walker is situated on the shores of Leech Lake, one of the largest lakes in the State. You will find ample facilities in Walker.

Parking, restrooms, water, picnic area, and shelter are on the north side of the trail in Akeley. One block from the trail is a huge Paul Bunyan statue at the municipal park on Main Street.

ROUTE SLIP	INCREMENT	TOTAL
Park Rapids		
Dorset	6.5	6.5
Nevis	5.0	11.5
Akeley	6.5	17.0
Walker	10.0	28.0
Walker Bay	3.0	31.0
Wilkinson	9.5	40.5
Cass Lake	9.0	49.5

MILE SCALE
0 1 2 3 4 5

Bicycle rentals, refreshments, and restrooms are available in most communities along the trail.

LEGEND

P Parking — 🎪 Picnic Area
🏕 Camping — 🍴 Refreshments
MF Multi-Facilities Available
Refreshments, First Aid — Lodging, Picnic — Telephone, Restrooms

——— Bicycle Trail (Paved)
- - - - Mountain Bike Trail (Natural)
-------- Alternate Use Trail
——— Roadway

Heartland State Trail

Itasca State Park

Trail Length	17.0 miles
Surface	Asphalt, roadway
Uses	Leisure bicycling, cross-country skiing, in-line skating, hiking
Location & Setting	Itasca State Park, where the Mississippi River begins, is a 32,000 acre park established in 1891. It is located 20 miles north of Park Rapids, on Hwy. 71. Heavily wooded, lakes.
Information	Itasca State Park Manager (218) 266-3654 Lake Itasca, MN 56460
Counties	Clearwater, Hubbard, Becker

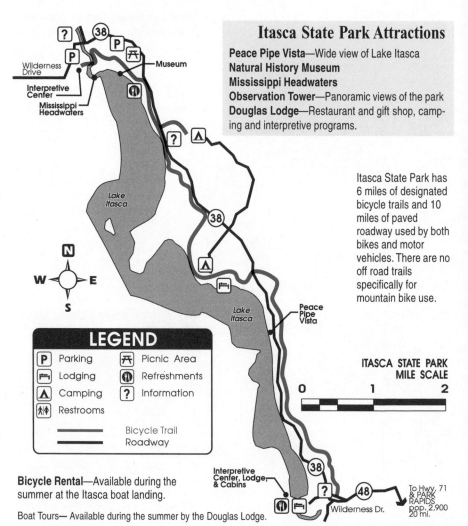

Itasca State Park Attractions

Peace Pipe Vista—Wide view of Lake Itasca
Natural History Museum
Mississippi Headwaters
Observation Tower—Panoramic views of the park
Douglas Lodge—Restaurant and gift shop, camping and interpretive programs.

Itasca State Park has 6 miles of designated bicycle trails and 10 miles of paved roadway used by both bikes and motor vehicles. There are no off road trails specifically for mountain bike use.

LEGEND

P	Parking	🎌	Picnic Area
🛏	Lodging	🍴	Refreshments
⛺	Camping	?	Information
🚻	Restrooms		
——	Bicycle Trail		
——	Roadway		

ITASCA STATE PARK MILE SCALE

0   1   2

Bicycle Rental—Available during the summer at the Itasca boat landing.

Boat Tours— Available during the summer by the Douglas Lodge.

Mi-GE-ZI Trail

Trail Length	18 miles
Surface	Asphalt - 8 to 10 feet wide
Uses	Leisure bicycling, cross-country skiing, in-line skating, hiking
Location & Setting	The MI-GE-ZI Trail winds around Pike Bay and the east side of Cass Lake on the Chippewa National Forest in north central Minnesota. It also connects to the Heartland State Trail 2 miles south of Cass Lake. The Trail runs along glittering lakes and through towering pine forests.
Information	USDA Forest Service, Walker Ranger District (218) 547-1044 HCR 73, Box 15 Walker, MN 56484
Counties	Hubbard

LEGEND

- **P** Parking
- **⊕** Refreshments
- **⚻** Restrooms
- **⚑** Camping
- ── Bicycle Trail
- ─ ─ Alternate Bike Trail
- ── Roadway

PENNINGTON

Knutson Dam

Mississippi River

Forest Rd. 2171

Sugar Lake

Cass Lake

Forest Rd. 2366

POTATO ISLANDS

STAR ISLAND

Forest Rd. 2171

Forest Rd. 2167

Forest Rd. 2348

Mississippi River

CEDAR ISLAND

CASS LAKE
pop. 950

Forest Rd. 2171

Forest Rd. 2352

Forest Rd. 2352

Strawberry Point

Grass Lake

SCHLEY

Isaacson Park

Forest Rd. 2133

Heartland Trail

Pike Bay

Forest Rd. 3910

Forest Rd. 2348

Sucker Lakes

Portage Lake

MILE SCALE
0   1   2   3

The MI-GE-ZI Trail was named in the Anishinabe language for the bald eagle.
At the time of this publication, paving of the trail is incomplete, but when completed it will become a major link in the 150 mile bike trail network including the Heartland and Paul Bunyan state trails.

Paul Bunyon State Trail

🚴 🎿 🛼 🏂 🏇

Trail Length	100 miles
Surface	see chart below
Uses	Leisure bicycling, cross-country skiing, in-line skating, snowmobiling, hiking
Location & Setting	North central Minnesota. Primarily located on abandoned rail grade, the trail links the towns of Brainerd, Walker and Bemidji plus several other small communities in route. It is generally level. Woods, lakes & open country.
Information	Minnesota Department of Natural Resources (218) 755-2265 Trails and Waterways Unit 2115 Birchmont Beach Road NE Bemidji, MN 56601
Counties	Crow Wing, Cass, Hubbard, Beltrami

FROM	SURFACE	WIDTH	LENGTH	MAP SYMBOL
Brainerd/Baxter to Hackensack	asphalt	10 feet wide	48.5 miles	A
Lake Bemidji to Mississippi River	asphalt	12 feet wide	5.3 miles	A
Walker to Hubard/Beltrami County line	ballast*	10 feet wide	28.0 miles	B
Hubbard/Betrami County line to Bemidji	ballast*	10 feet wide	18.0 miles	B

asphalt planned

Mileage Guide

	INCREMENT	TOTALS
Baxter		100.0
Merrifield	9.0	9.0 ..... 91.0
Nisswa	5.8	14.8 ..... 85.2
Pequot Lakes	6.2	21.0 ..... 79.0
Jenkins	3.0	24.0 ..... 76.0
Pine River	6.0	30.0 ..... 70.0
Backus	8.8	38.8 ..... 61.2
Elackensack	7.6	46.4 ..... 53.6
Walker	16.8	63.2 ..... 36.8
Benedict	7.8	71.0 ..... 29.0
Laporte	5.2	76.2 ..... 23.8
Guthrie	6.2	82.4 ..... 17.6
Nary	5.2	87.6 ..... 12.4
Bemidji	9.6	97.2 ..... 2.8
Lake Bemidji SP	2.8	100.0

Crow Wing State Park

Phone: (218) 829-8022
7100 State Park Rd SW,
Brainerd, MN 56401
The historic Red River Ox Cart Trail goes through the once prosperous town of Old Crow Wing. Park visitors will enjoy the natural beauty of the confluence of the Crow Wing and Mississippi Rivers. Hike the 18 mi of trails to capture a sense of the area's history. 6.4 mi of cross-country ski. Year round. 8am-10pm daily. Park permits: $18 annual, $4 daily. Located 9 mi S of Brainerd on Hwy 371. Park headquarters 1 mi west of 371 on Co Rd 27.

Parking Available in Baxter, Merrifield, Nisswa, Pequot Lakes, Jenkins, Pine River, Backus, Hackensack and Walker.

The south trailhead is located in Baxter. From Brainerd, go west on Highway 210 about 3/4 of a mile. Turn north (right) on Highway 371 to the first stoplight (Excelsior Road). Turn east (right), and continue to the parking lot.

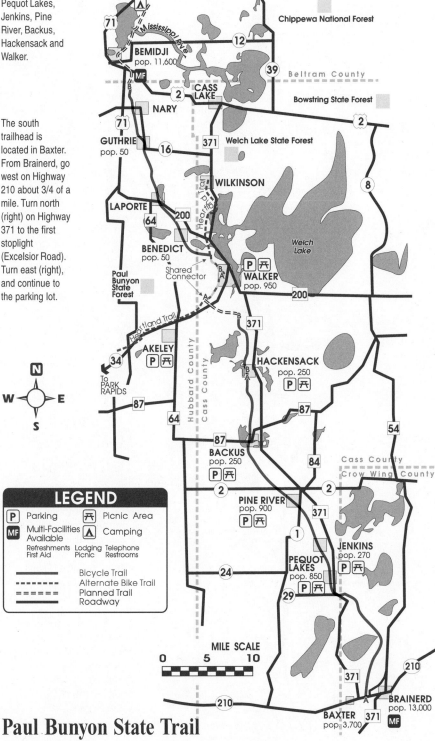

LEGEND

P	Parking	**⛱**	Picnic Area
MF	Multi-Facilities Available	**Ⓐ**	Camping

Refreshments Lodging Telephone
First Aid   Picnic   Restrooms

———————— Bicycle Trail
- - - - - - Alternate Bike Trail
====== Planned Trail
———— Roadway

MILE SCALE
0   5   10

Paul Bunyon State Trail

Willard Munger State Trail System

Western Waterfront Trail
Alex Laveau Trail
Willard Munger State Trail
Sunrise Prairie Trail
Hardwood Creek Trail
Gateway Trail
(East Metro Section)

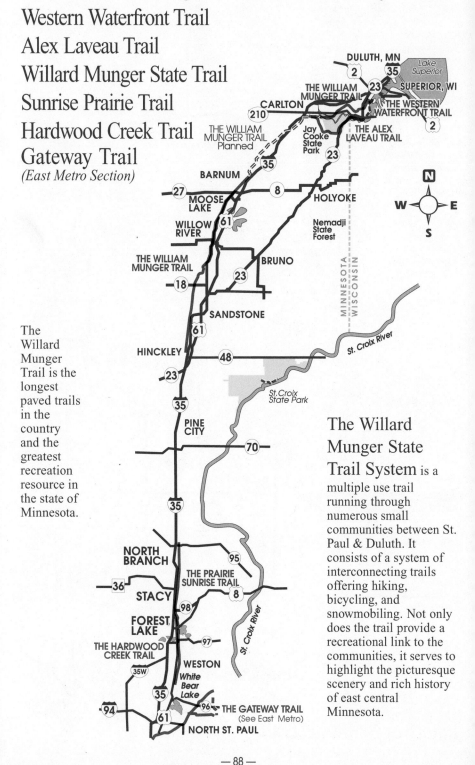

The Willard Munger Trail is the longest paved trails in the country and the greatest recreation resource in the state of Minnesota.

The Willard Munger State Trail System is a multiple use trail running through numerous small communities between St. Paul & Duluth. It consists of a system of interconnecting trails offering hiking, bicycling, and snowmobiling. Not only does the trail provide a recreational link to the communities, it serves to highlight the picturesque scenery and rich history of east central Minnesota.

Western Waterfront Trail 🚲🚶

Trail Length	5.0 miles
Surface	Paved for about a mile; rest is screenings
Uses	Leisure bicycling, hiking
Location & Setting	Located south of Duluth proper, bordering the west side of Spirit Lake and the St. Louis River. It connects to the Willard Munger Trail at its north trailhead and Commonwealth Avenue at its south trailhead.
Information	Duluth Parks & Recreation Department (218) 723-3337
Counties	Carlton

DULUTH
pop. 84,493

Gasser Park

SCANLON

ESKO

Snively Park

Western Waterfront Trail

Morgan Park

Ely's Peak

Western Waterfront Trail

Spirit Lake

Willard Munder Trail

Fond Du Lac Park

Merrit Park

Oldenburg Point

Carson Park

Birchwood Park

OLIVER

St. Louis River

CARLTON
pop. 923

Jay Cooke State Park

Leimer Rd.

Commonwealth

Alex Laveau Trail

MN State Line

WI State Line

WRENSHALL

MILE SCALE
0 1 2 3

N
W —✦— E
S

Alex Laveau Trail 🚲🎿🛼🚶

Trail Length	16 miles, including 10 miles of designated shoulder
Surface	Asphalt: 6 miles plus paved shoulder
Uses	Leisure bicycling, cross-country skiing, in-line skating, hiking
Location & Setting	From Carlton southeast through Wrenshall to Hwy. 23. North on Hwy. 23, along a designated shoulder to Hwy. 105 south of Duluth.
Information	Munger Trail Towns Association (218) 485-8836 205 Elm Avenue—P.O. Box 110 Moose Lake, MN 55767
Counties	Carlton, St. Louis

LEGEND

- **P** Parking
- **Picnic Area**
- **Shelter**
- **Restrooms**
- **MF** Multi-Facilities Available
- **Camping**

Refreshments / First Aid   Lodging / Picnic   Telephone / Restrooms

------- Bicycle Trail
- - - - - Alternate Bike Trail
- - - - - Alternate Use Trail
====== Planned Trail
        Roadway

N W E S

Duluth Area Attractions

Lakewalk—A mile plus boardwalk and bicycle trail from Canal Park to 26th Avenue E. along the lake shore.

Fitger's Brewery Complex—Shops and restaurants along the lake shore with bike and carriage paths.

The Depot—506 W. Michigan St. • Houses 3 museums, visual arts, and 4 performing groups.

Marine Museum and Canal Park Visitor Center—Interpretive geologic and maritime exhibits.

Hinckley Area Attractions

Hinckley Fire Museum—Features logging and railroad exhibits, and the restored Depot Agent's office and living quarters.

Hinckley Flea Market—Highway 48 East • Midwest's largest indoor/outdoor Flea Market.

ATKINSON
MAHTOWA
Match Line
61
35
Wayside
BARNUM pop. 464
4.0 mi
73
8
27
MOOSE LAKE pop. 1206
Moose Lake State Park
27
6.0 mi
35
61
STURGEON LAKE pop. 222
Sturgeon Lake
DUQUETTE
General Andrews State Forest
46
KERRICK
4.5 mi
WILLOW RIVER pop. 303
Wayside
43
RUTLEDGE pop. 185
4.5 mi
BRUNO
33
61
5.5 mi
23
33
DAR Mem. State Forest
FINLAYSON pop. 202
18
35
Wayside
61
GRONINGEN
3.5 mi
28
Banning State Park
ASKOV
61
SANDSTONE

South Trailhead-Exit I-35 at Hinckley and go west to old Highway 61. Turn north and continue to County Rd. 18; turn west across tracks to parking lot. The trailhead is within a block of a Dairy Queen and a gas station. There are restaurants, lodging, restrooms and picnic facilities in the area.

FRIESLAND 26
4.5 mi
35
4.5 mi
61

MILE SCALE
0 1 2 3 4 5

HINCKLEY pop. 946
18 Wayside
48
St. Croix State Park

Willard Munger State Trail

Willard Munger State Trail

Trail Length 76.0 miles (including 3 planned miles)

Surface Asphalt

Uses Leisure bicycling, cross-country skiing, in-line skating, snowmobiling, hiking

Location & Setting The trail currently extends from Hinckley to Duluth, but will eventually run all the way from St. Paul to Duluth through a series of interconnecting trails. The trail is laid on an old railbed, asphalt surface, and largely flat with scattered forest, trees, and considerable farmland. The sections from Carlton to Duluth provides views of the St. Louis River, forest area, and rock cuts.

Information Munger Trail Town Association (218) 485-8836
205 Elm Avenue
P.O. Box 110
Moose Lake, MN 55767

Counties Pine, Carlton

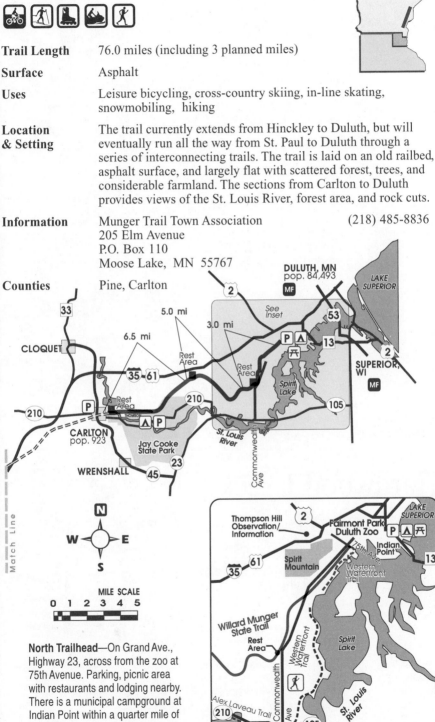

North Trailhead—On Grand Ave., Highway 23, across from the zoo at 75th Avenue. Parking, picnic area with restaurants and lodging nearby. There is a municipal campground at Indian Point within a quarter mile of the trail and on the St. Louis River.

Sunrise Prairie Trail

Trail Length 15.0 miles: 10 feet wide plus parallel dirt path

Surface Paved

Uses Leisure bicycling, cross-country skiing, in-line skating, hiking

Location & Setting The trail is located in Chisago County and runs from just north of Forest Lake to North Branch. It continues parallel to Highway 61.

Information Chisago County Parks Dept.
36894 Tanger Drive
North Branch, MN 55056
(612) 674-2345

Counties Chisago County

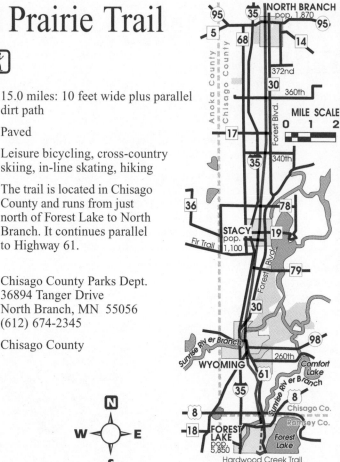

Hardwood Creek Trail

Trail Length 9.6 miles: 10 feet wide plus parallel dirt path

Surface Paved

Uses Leisure bicycling, cross-country skiing, in-line skating, hiking

Location & Setting The trail is located In Washington County and runs between Hugo and Forest Lake. It closely parallels Highway 61.

Counties Washington

Soo Line Trail

🚴	🎿	🛼	🚶	

Trail Length	11.0 miles, plus 8 miles planned
Surface	Paved, 8 feet wide
Uses	Leisure bicycling, cross-country skiing, in-line skating, hiking
Location & Setting	The 10 parallel path is open to A.T.V.'s and snowmobiling. The Trail extends from Onomia to Isle, south of Mill Lacs Lake, along the former Soo Line railroad grade, and passes through the village of Wahkon. It meanders through forest, farmland and wetlands.
Information	Mill Lacs County (320) 983-8201 565 Eighth Street NE Milaca, MN 56353
Counties	Mill Lacs

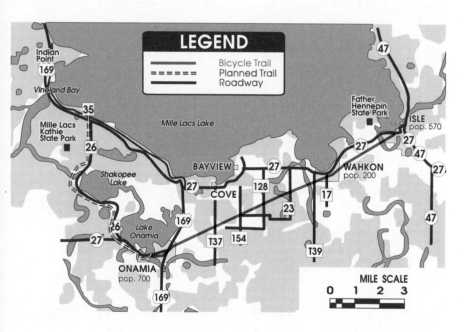

Father Hennepin State Park and Kathio State Park are both easily accessible from both ends of the trail. Father Hennepin State Park is linked via low volume city street in Isle. Kathio State Park, five miles north west of Onamia, is linked via County State Aid Highway 26 which also has a relatively low traffic volume.

The bike trail is within a duel use corridor. There is also a ten foot unpaved portion for A.T.V. users that parallels the bike trail.

Onamia is renovating a depot into a rest stop along the trail. There is an exhibit, the 'Ellen Ruth" a former Mille Lacs Lake Launch, which is only one block from the trail.

St. Croix State Park

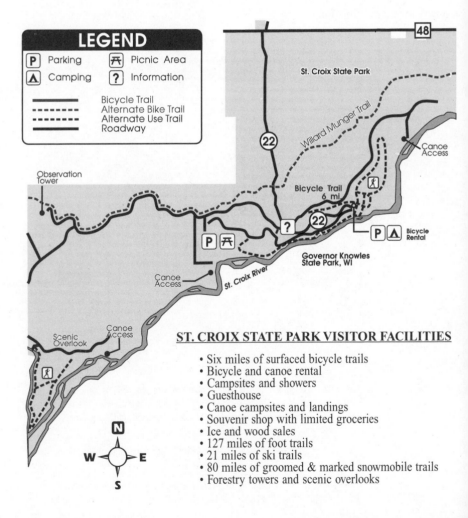

Trail Length	6.0 miles
Surface	Paved
Uses	Leisure bicycling, cross-country skiing, in-line skating, hiking
Location & Setting	St. Croix State Park borders the St. Croix River and Wisconsin state line and is located approximately 60 miles north of the Twin Cities and 15 miles east of Hinckley. It is the largest state park in Minnesota with over 33,000 acres of forest, meadows and streams.
Information	St. Croix State Park (612) 384-6591
Counties	Pine

LEGEND

- **P** Parking
- **⚑** Picnic Area
- **▲** Camping
- **?** Information

— Bicycle Trail
---- Alternate Bike Trail
---- Alternate Use Trail
— Roadway

St. Croix State Park

Willard Munger Trail

Observation Tower

Bicycle Trail 6 mi

Canoe Access

Governor Knowles State Park, WI

Bicycle Rental

St. Croix River

Canoe Access

Scenic Overlook

Canoe Access

N / **W** / **E** / **S**

ST. CROIX STATE PARK VISITOR FACILITIES

- Six miles of surfaced bicycle trails
- Bicycle and canoe rental
- Campsites and showers
- Guesthouse
- Canoe campsites and landings
- Souvenir shop with limited groceries
- Ice and wood sales
- 127 miles of foot trails
- 21 miles of ski trails
- 80 miles of groomed & marked snowmobile trails
- Forestry towers and scenic overlooks

Index

City	Trail Name	Page
Elysian	Sakatah Singing Hills State Trail	26
Excelsior	LRT Trail	67
Faribault	River Bend Nature Center	18
	Sakatah Singing Hills State Trail	26
Finlayson	Willard Munger State Trail	90
Forest Lake	Hardwood Creek Trail	92
	Sunrise Prairie Trail	92
Fountain	Root River State Trail	22
Fridley	Anoka County Riverfront Park	56
	Rice Creek West Regional Trail	56
Friesland	Willard Munger State Trail	90
Greenfield	Lake Rebecca Park Reserve	51
Greenwood	LRT Trail	67
Groningen	Willard Munger State Trail	90
Guthrie	Paul Bunyan State Trail	86
Hackensack	Paul Bunyan State Trail	86
Harmony	Harmony-Preston Valley State Trail	22
	Root River State Trail	22
Hawick	Glacial Lakes State Trail	16
Hinckley	Saint Croix State Park	94
	Willard Munger State Trail	90
Hopkins	LRT Trail	67
Hugo	Hardwood Creek Trail	92
Hutchinson	Luce Line State Trail	52
Independence	Baker Park Reserve	46
	Lake Rebecca Park Reserve	51
	Luce Line State Trail	52
Isinours Junction	Root River State Trail	22
Isle	Soo Line Trail	93
Jenkins	Paul Bunyan State Trail	86
Lanesboro	Root River State Trail	22
LaPorte	Paul Bunyan State Trail	86
Lyndale	Luce Line State Trail	52
Madison Lake	Sakatah Singing Hills State Trail	26
Mankato	Red Jacket Trail	15
	Sakatah Singing Hills State Trail	26
Mantowa	Willard Munger State Trail	90
Maple Grove	Elm Creek Park Reserve	48
	Hennepin Trail Corridor	50

City to Trail Index *(Continued)*

County to Trail Index

County to Trail Index (Continued)

Mountain Biking Trails in Minnesota
Suggested Opportunities

SOUTHEAST MINNESOTA

MYRE BIG ISLAND STATE PARK

Length	5.8 miles
Surface	Grassy
Effort Level	Easy
Setting	Rolling hills, shallow lakes and marshes
Location	Three miles southeast of Albert Lea.
Park Office	(507) 373-5084

RICHARD J. DORER MEMORIAL STATE FOREST
SNAKE CREEK UNIT

Length	8.0 miles
Surface	Grassy and packed dirt
Effort Level	Moderate
Setting	Snake Creek runs through a valley. A rough topography with slopes rising 300 feet on either side. Climbs follow reasonable grades, area is forested.
Location	Four miles south of Kellogg of Hwy. 61.
Unit Office	612/345-3216

TROUT VALLEY UNIT

Length	7.4 miles
Surface	Packed dirt, rocky hills
Effort Level	Easy to moderate
Setting	Trout Valley includes steep, wooded ridges and bluffs. The ridge tops are open agricultural land and the slopes wooded. The trail connects the valley with the ridge top.
Location	Fourteen miles northwest of Winona off Hwy. 61 or 13 miles southeast of Wabash off Hwy. 61.
Unit Office	507/523-2183

BRONK UNIT

Length	7.0 miles
Surface	Packed dirt
Effort Level	Moderate
Setting	Trail consists of two loops, which follow the edge of the woods as they go around a ridge.
Location	From Winona, take Hwy. 14 west to Hwy. 23 in Stockton, then north 2.1 miles to Hillsdale Township Rd. #6. East .5 miles to the parking lot.
Unit Office	507/523-2183

MINNEAPOLIS/ST. PAUL AREA

ELM CREEK PARK RESERVE

Length	5.0 miles
Surface	Grassy
Effort Level	Easy
Setting	Hilly
Location	Northwest of Osseo on County Road 81 to Territorial Road. Look for sign on the right.
Park Office	612/424-5511

MURPHY-HANREHAN PARK RESERVE

Length	6.0 miles
Surface	Grassy
Effort Level	Moderate to difficult
Setting	Terrain within the park is rugged with a number of steep hills. The trail is a loop on hilly ski trails.
Location	Near Prior Lake on Scott County Road 75.
Park Office	612/447-6913

MOUND SPRINGS

Length	3.3 miles, plus additional trails
Surface	Packed dirt, sand, grass
Effort Level	Moderate
Setting	River bottom, wooded areas and some steep hills. Urban.
Location	Bloomington.
Phone	612/998-8877

LEBANON HILLS REGIONAL PARK - WEST

Length	2.5 miles
Surface	Dirt and grass
Effort Level	Moderate
Setting	Hilly. Located in deep hardwoods
Location	Hwy. 35E south from St. Paul to Cliff Road. East to Johnny Cake Ridge Rd., then about ¼ mile south.
Park Office	612/437-6608

MN VALLEY TRAIL STATE PARK — LOUISVILLE SWAMP

Length	19.5 miles
Surface	Grass and dirt
Effort Level	Easy to moderate
Setting	Parallels the Minnesota River. Lowlands subject to frequent flooding.
Location	About 4 miles southwest of Shakopee. From Hwy. 169 take 145th St. for ½ mile. Follow signs.
Park Office	612/492-6400

Length	13.5 miles
Surface	Grass and dirt
Effort Level	Easy
Setting	Wetlands, wooded areas, prairie, savanna uplands.
Location	North on County Road 9 for a quarter mile from Hwy. 169 in Jordan. Left on County Road 57 for 4 miles to entrance.
Park Office	612/492-6400

NORTHERN MINNESOTA

SAVANNA PORTAGE STATE PARK

Length	12.0 miles
Surface	Grass, dirt roads, single track
Effort Level	Easy to moderate
Setting	Rolling hills and sandy soil.
Location	From Minneapolis take Hwy. 65 north approximately 125 miles to County Road 14. Northeast 10 miles to park entrance.
Park Office	218/426-3271

JAY COOKE STATE PARK

Length	12.0 miles
Surface	Grassy, rocks, some paved
Effort Level	Moderate
Setting	Massive rock formations, hardwood forest, steep valleys. Beautiful views of the St. Louis River.
Location	12 miles west of Duluth on Hwy. 210. From the twin cities, take Hwy. 35W north to the Carlton exit at Hwy. 210. East for 5 miles to the park entrance.
Park Office	218/384-4610

SAINT CROIX STATE FOREST

Length	18.0 miles
Surface	Gravel, sand, grass, rocks, dirt road
Effort Level	Moderate
Setting	Quite variable, from flat gravel, through woods, rolling to steep hills that are often sandy and rocky as well as dirt road.
Location	Hwy. 48 approximately 22 miles east of Hinckley to Danbury.
Park Office	218/485-4474

SAINT CROIX STATE PARK

Length	13.0 miles
Surface	Grassy
Effort Level	Easy to moderate
Setting	Forests, meadows, marshes and streams
	St. Croix is the largest state park in Minnesota
Location	Take Hwy. 48 approximately 15 miles east of Hinckley to CR22 and the park entrance. Proceed south.
Park Office	612/384-6591

PILLSBURY STATE FOREST

Length	27.0 miles
Surface	Grassy and dirt
Effort Level	Moderate to difficult
Setting	Rolling to hilly with numerous small ponds and lakes.
Location	From Brainerd, go north and then west on CR 77 for approximately 10 miles. Turn southwest on Pillager Forest Rd. for 2 miles. Trailhead is on the west side.
Forest Office	218/828-2565

FRENCH RAPIDS TRAIL

Length	7.5 miles
Surface	Grass and dirt
Effort Level	Moderate to difficult
Setting	Hilly, wooded. There are sandy sections and steep climbs. The trail is not well marked.
Location	Northeast on Hwy 210 from Brainerd to airport exit (Hwy. 142). Turn left and drive 2.5 miles to an unmarked road. Turn lef to dead-end.
Chamber	218/829-2838

LAKE BEMIDJI STATE PARK

Length	9.0 miles
Surface	Grassy
Effort Level	Easy
Setting	Pine-moraine, rolling topography with swamps and bogs.
Location	1.7 miles off County Road 21, 5 miles north of Bemidji. Entrance to the park is from County Hwy. 20.
Park Office	218/755-3843

SUGAR HILLS TRAIL

Length	12.0 miles
Surface	Grassy and hard-packed, frequently following old logging roads
Effort Level	Moderate to difficult
Setting	Hilly, with many peaks, valleys, and ridges.
Location	South on Hwy. 169 for 7 miles from Grand Rapids. West on CR17 for 2 miles to County Road 449, and continue west for another 3 miles.
Contact	218/327-1462 (Ruttger's Sugarlake Lodge)

PAUL BUNYAN STATE FOREST

Length	32.0 miles
Surface	Dirt and forest roads
Effort Level	Moderate to difficult
Setting	Forest, ponds, bogs, and some marshy areas.
Location	From Akeley, proceed 10 miles north on Hwy. 64 to Forest Rd 2.
	The town of Akeley is between Walker and Park Rapids.
Park Office	218/732-3309

LAND O'LAKES STATE FOREST

Length	15.0 miles
Surface	Grassy, dirt
Effort Level	Easy to moderate
Setting	Rolling hills, forest, lakes, small ponds
Location	North of Outing on Hwy. 6 to County Road 48, then west 1 mile to trailhead on north side of road.
Forest Office	218/568-4566

PINCUSHION MOUNTAIN

Length	15.0 miles
Surface	Grassy, dirt
Effort Level	Moderate
Setting	Forest, lowlands, bluffs, several footbridges.
Location	From Grand Marais, 2 miles north on CR 12. Grand Marais is approximately 110 miles northeast of Duluth on Hwy. 61.
Information	218/387-1750

NORTHERN MINNESOTA *(Continued)*

WHITEFISH LAKE

Length	20 miles
Surface	Rocky
Effort Level	Easy to difficult
Setting	The trail skirts several lakes, ponds, and marshes. Rolling terrain and wooded areas.
Location	Northwest of Tofte, which is approximately 90 miles northeast of Duluth on Hwy. 61. From Tofte take FR 343 north to FR 166, then left to FR 346. North to FR 170, left to FR 357 and then north.
Information	218/663-7981

GEGOKA/FLATHORN

Length	98 miles of loops
Surface	Old forest roads
Effort Level	Easy to moderate
Setting	Varied. Woods, wetlands, lakes, ponds. Rolling forest roads and some rocky hills. Forests are largely pine, birch aspen, and maple.
Location	Approximately 60 miles northeast of Duluth to Hwy. 1. Northwest on Hwy. 1 about 6 miles past Isabella.
Information	218/323-7676

SPLIT ROCK LIGHTHOUSE STATE PARK

Length	8.0 miles
Surface	Grass and gravel
Effort Level	Easy to Moderate
Setting	Rugged Lake Superior shoreline. Trail course varies from woods, open flat country to bumpy, loose rock and steeply pitched areas.
Location	Hwy. 61, 20 miles northeast of Two Harbors, approximately 45 miles from Duluth.
Park Office	218/226-3065

GOOSEBERRY FALLS STATE PARK

Length	12.0 miles
Surface	Grassy
Effort Level	Moderate
Setting	Forests, Lake Superior shoreline, five waterfalls, Gooseberry River. Conifer, aspen, and birch forests.
Location	Approximately 35 miles north of Duluth on Hwy. 61.
Park Office	218/834-3855

SCENIC STATE PARK

Length	5 miles designated (18 miles total)
Surface	Maintained ski trails - both single and double track
Effort Level	Easy to moderate
Setting	Rolling terrain, flat areas, and woods. There are several magnificent stands of old white and red pine. The park encompasses Coon and Sandwick Lakes.
Location	From Bigfork, take County Road 7 south and then east a total of 7 miles to park entrance.
Park Office	218/743-3362

McCARTHY BEACH STATE PARK

Length	15.0 miles
Surface	Grassy with both single and double track
Effort Level	Moderate
Setting	Deeply wooded with rolling hills and small valleys. The trails follow the ridge tops of the park's moraines.
Location	Hwy. 169 north of Hibbing to County Road 5 and north 15 miles to the park entrance.
Park Office	218/254-2411

BIG ASPEN TRAILS

Length	10.0 miles
Surface	Hard packed dirt and grass
Effort Level	Easy to difficult
Setting	A large treadway that passes through large pine and hardwood forest. It uses both recent logging roads and old railroad grades.
Location	From Virginia take Hwy. 53 north for 8 miles to County Road 131.Proceed northeast for 1 mile, then west on County Road 68 for .3 miles to County Road 405. North on 405 for 2 miles to parking lot.
Forest Office	218/229-3371

GIANT RIDGE TRAILS

Location	Hwy. 135, 1.5 miles from Biwabik to County Road 138 north. Turn left and drive 3 miles. Look for signs.
Information	800/688-SNOW

NORTHERN MINNESOTA *(Continued)*

LAURENTIAN TRAIL

Length	5.5 miles
Surface	Grassy, gravel
Effort Level	Easy to moderate
Setting	Ski trail is grassy with moderate hills. The snowmobile trail is largely gravel with moderate hills. Look out for protruding or loose boulders. There are some bike signs.

SILVER TRAIL

Length	6.0 miles
Surface	Well maintained ski trails
Effort Level	Moderate to difficult
Setting	Rolling terrain, thick woods, nearby lakes

WYNNE LAKE OVERLOOK

Length	10.0 miles
Surface	Well maintained ski and snowmobile trails
Effort Level	Moderate
Setting	Woods, ridges, panoramic views of Embarrass Lake, Sabin Lake, Wynne Lake and Superior National Forest. Some hills and rocky areas.

To order additional copies of this book:

Pay by Check or Credit Card

Mail Check to:

American Bike Trails
1157 South Milwaukee Avenue
Libertyville, IL 60048

Book *(per copy)* $12.95
Handling *(per order)* $2.00
Sales Tax—IL residents *(per copy)*.........$.85
TOTAL   **$15.80**

To order by Credit Card call (800) 246-4627

American Bike Trails
publishes and distributes maps, books and guides
for the recreational bicyclist. Our trail maps
cover over 350 trails throughout the states of
Illinois, Iowa, Michigan, Minnesota and Wisconsin.

For a free copy of our catalog write to the above address